The Art of Grant Proposals

Winning Strategies for Nonprofit Success

Courtney Alexis

© Copyright 2024 - All rights reserved.

The content contained within this book may not be reproduced, duplicated or transmitted without direct written permission from the author or the publisher.

Under no circumstances will any blame or legal responsibility be held against the publisher, or author, for any damages, reparation, or monetary loss due to the information contained within this book, either directly or indirectly.

Legal Notice:

This book is copyright protected. It is only for personal use. You cannot amend, distribute, sell, use, quote or paraphrase any part, or the content within this book, without the consent of the author or publisher.

Disclaimer Notice:

Please note the information contained within this document is for educational and entertainment purposes only. All effort has been executed to present accurate, up to date, reliable, complete information. No warranties of any kind are declared or implied. Readers acknowledge that the author is not engaged in the rendering of legal, financial, medical or professional advice. The content within this book has been derived from various sources. Please consult a licensed professional before attempting any techniques outlined in this book.

By reading this document, the reader agrees that under no circumstances is the author responsible for any losses, direct or indirect, that are incurred as a result of the use of the information contained within this document, including, but not limited to, errors, omissions, or inaccuracies.

Table of Contents

INTRODUCTION 1

CHAPTER 1: UNDERSTANDING GRANT OPPORTUNITIES 5
   RESEARCHING AND IDENTIFYING RELEVANT GRANT OPPORTUNITIES 5
      Understand Your Needs and Goals 6
      Start With Online Databases and Resources 6
      Use Keywords Effectively 6
      Explore Local Resources 7
      Network and Seek Recommendations 7
      Review Funder Priorities and Past Grants 7
      Attend Grant Workshops and Webinars 7
      Keep Track and Stay Organized 8
      Be Realistic and Selective 8
   ASSESSING ELIGIBILITY CRITERIA AND ALIGNMENT WITH ORGANIZATIONAL GOALS 9
      Understand the Funder's Requirements 9
      Match With Your Organizational Goals 10
      Assess Your Capacity 10
      Consider Restrictions and Conditions 10
      Make a Go/No-Go Decision 11
      Practical Steps 11
   BUILDING RELATIONSHIPS WITH GRANTMAKERS AND FUNDERS 11
      Do Your Homework 12
      Do an Introduction 12
      Attend Events and Workshops 12
      Be Authentic and Transparent 13
      Communicate Regularly 13
      Invite Funders to Visit 13
      Show Gratitude 14
      Seek Feedback 14
      Foster Long-Term Relationships 14

CHAPTER 2: CRAFTING A COMPELLING PROPOSAL NARRATIVE 15
   DEVELOPING THE PROJECT DESCRIPTION 16
      Articulating Clear Objectives 16
      Outlining Your Methods 16
      Demonstrating Anticipated Impact 18
      Tips for Crafting Your Project Description 19

ASSESSING ELIGIBILITY CRITERIA AND ALIGNMENT WITH ORGANIZATIONAL GOALS............19
   Understanding Eligibility Criteria..20
   Ensuring Alignment With Organizational Goals..20
   Conducting a Thorough Assessment..21
   Strategic Grant Management: A Framework for Success.............................22
BUILDING RELATIONSHIPS WITH GRANTMAKERS AND FUNDERS...............................22
   Understanding the Significance of Relationships...23
   Steps to Build Strong Relationships..23
TIPS FOR SUSTAINING RELATIONSHIPS..25

CHAPTER 3: BUDGETING AND FINANCIAL PLANNING 27

CREATING A REALISTIC AND COMPREHENSIVE PROJECT BUDGET..............................28
   The Importance of a Comprehensive Budget...28
   Steps to Creating a Realistic Budget...28
   Example of a Project Budget..31
   Best Tips for Budget Presentation..32
JUSTIFYING BUDGET ITEMS AND EXPENSES...33
   Understanding the Importance of Justification...33
   Steps to Justify Budget Items..33
   Best Practices for Effective Justification..36
DEMONSTRATING FINANCIAL SUSTAINABILITY AND ACCOUNTABILITY......................37
   Financial Sustainability..37
   Financial Accountability...39
   Integrating Sustainability and Accountability in Your Grant Proposal.........40

CHAPTER 4: DEMONSTRATING ORGANIZATIONAL CAPACITY AND EFFECTIVENESS... 43

HIGHLIGHTING THE ORGANIZATION'S TRACK RECORD AND ACCOMPLISHMENTS.................44
   Understanding the Importance..44
   Mission Alignment..44
   Quantifiable Outcomes...45
   Success Stories and Testimonials..45
   Awards and Recognition...45
   Partnerships and Collaborations..46
   Financial Stewardship...46
   Structuring Your Accomplishments..47
SHOWCASING ORGANIZATIONAL CAPACITY AND CAPABILITIES................................49
   Organizational Capacity..49
   Organizational Capabilities..50
   Enhancing Capacity and Capabilities..52
PROVIDING EVIDENCE OF PAST SUCCESS AND IMPACT...52
   Importance of Evidence of Past Success..53
   Types of Evidence...53
   How to Present Evidence..54

CHAPTER 5: ADDRESSING EVALUATION AND IMPACT MEASUREMENT 57

Developing a Robust Evaluation Plan to Measure Project Outcomes 58
- Defining Clear Objectives and Goals 58
- Identifying Key Performance Indicators 58
- Choosing the Right Evaluation Methods 59
- Developing Data Collection Tools 59
- Establishing a Data Collection Timeline 59
- Ensuring Data Quality and Integrity 60
- Analyzing and Interpreting Data 60
- Reporting Findings 60
- Using Findings for Improvement 60

Identifying Relevant Performance Indicators and Metrics 61
- Understand the Project's Goals and Objectives 61
- Engage Stakeholders 61
- Categorize Indicators 61
- Select Specific, Relevant Indicators 62
- Ensure Measurability and Feasibility 62
- Align With Industry Standards and Best Practices 63
- Use a Balanced Approach 63
- Regularly Review and Update Indicators 63
- Establish Baselines and Targets 63
- Document and Communicate the Indicators 64

Communicating the Potential Impact and Significance of the Proposed Project . 64
- Understanding the Issue 64
- Articulating the Vision and Goals 65
- Using Data and Evidence 65
- Sharing Stories of Change 65
- Highlighting the Broader Impact 66
- Building Trust and Credibility 66
- Engaging and Mobilizing Supporters 66

CHAPTER 6: WRITING STYLE AND PRESENTATION 67

Writing Clear, Concise, and Persuasive Grant Proposals 68
- Clarity in Objectives and Goals 68
- Conciseness in Language 68
- Persuasive Storytelling 69
- Detailed Budget and Justification 69
- Evidence of Need and Impact 70
- Strong Organizational Capability 70
- Clear Evaluation Plan 71

Formatting and Structuring the Proposal for Maximum Impact 71
- Title Page 71
- Executive Summary 72

- Problem Statement ... 73
- Goals and Objectives ... 73
- Project Description ... 74
- Budget ... 75
- Evaluation Plan ... 75
- Organizational Capability ... 76
- Conclusion ... 77
- EDITING AND PROOFREADING FOR ACCURACY AND PROFESSIONALISM ... 78
  - Review for Clarity and Consistency ... 78
  - Check for Grammar and Spelling Errors ... 78
  - Verify Data and Facts ... 78
  - Maintain a Professional Tone and Language ... 79
  - Consistency in Formatting ... 79
  - Logical Flow and Structure ... 79
  - Proofreading Techniques ... 79
  - Use the Track Changes Feature ... 79
  - Peer Review ... 80
  - Checklist for Final Review ... 81

CHAPTER 7: SUBMISSION AND FOLLOW-UP ... 83

- REVIEWING SUBMISSION GUIDELINES AND REQUIREMENTS ... 84
  - Carefully Read the Request for Proposal or Request for Application ... 84
  - Eligibility Criteria ... 84
  - Funding Priorities and Objectives ... 85
  - Application Components ... 85
  - Formatting Requirements ... 85
  - Submission Process ... 85
  - Deadlines ... 86
  - Additional Review and Checklist ... 86
  - Final Review ... 86
- ASSEMBLING AND SUBMITTING THE GRANT PROPOSAL PACKAGE ... 87
  - Gather Required Documents ... 87
  - Format and Organize the Documents ... 88
  - Review for Completeness and Accuracy ... 88
  - Prepare for Submission ... 89
  - Confirm Submission ... 89
  - Follow Up ... 90
  - Maintain Records ... 90
- FOLLOWING UP WITH FUNDERS AND MAINTAINING COMMUNICATION ... 90

CHAPTER 8: OVERCOMING COMMON CHALLENGES AND PITFALLS ... 93

- ADDRESSING COMMON CHALLENGES AND OBSTACLES IN GRANT WRITING ... 93
  - Understanding Funder Requirements ... 93
  - Developing a Clear and Compelling Narrative ... 94

- *Demonstrating Impact and Sustainability* 94
- *Competition and Limited Funding* 94
- *Time Management* 94
- STRATEGIES FOR NAVIGATING REJECTION AND LEARNING FROM FEEDBACK 95
- TIPS FOR STAYING MOTIVATED AND RESILIENT 96

CHAPTER 9: CASE STUDIES AND EXAMPLES 99

- REAL-WORLD EXAMPLES OF SUCCESSFUL GRANT PROPOSALS 99
  - *Community Health Initiative* 99
  - *Environmental Conservation Effort* 100
- LESSONS LEARNED AND INSIGHTS FROM GRANT-WRITING EXPERIENCES 104

CONCLUSION: MASTERING THE ART OF GRANT PROPOSALS 105

REFERENCES 109

Introduction

Securing funding is a crucial yet challenging aspect of nonprofit management. For many organizations, grant proposals become the lifeblood that upholds their missions, fuels their initiatives or programs, and multiplies their impact. The art of creating a compelling grant proposal is a vital skill that, once mastered, can help you unlock a plethora of opportunities and resources, driving your nonprofit toward its goals.

Welcome to *The Art of Grant Proposals: Winning Strategies for Nonprofit Success*, where you will familiarize yourself with the art of grant proposals. This guide is tailored to equip you with the tools, confidence, and knowledge to navigate the intricate world of grant writing. Whether you are a newbie in the world of grants or looking to polish your approach, I aim to support you at each step of the way. I am Courtney Alexis, a nonprofit professional with over 20 years of experience in fundraising, strategic planning, and organizational development.

Throughout my career, I have been committed to helping nonprofits succeed by empowering them with effective fundraising methods and tools. I have also served in leadership roles for many nonprofit organizations, guiding them to attain their fundraising objectives and make a positive and lasting impact in their communities. I believe that a blend of creativity, expertise, and compassion will help you in not only understanding but also overcoming the challenges that you will face on this journey.

At its core, a grant proposal goes beyond mere requests for funds; it is a compelling narrative that tells the story of your nonprofit, highlights its triumphs, and its vision for the future. It is also an opportunity to connect with funders on a profound level, to illustrate the amazing and unique value of your work, and to cultivate lasting partnerships.

Creating this narrative requires a blend of meticulous planning, persuasive communication, and strategic thinking.

Throughout this book, we will explore critical parts of a successful grant proposal, such as comprehending funder priorities, conducting thorough research, crafting a persuasive case for support, and adhering to the distinct requirements of every funding opportunity. You will learn many practical insights and expert tips as well as get a behind-the-scenes look at what will make your proposals stand out.

Embarking on this grant-writing journey can be quite daunting, but know that every successful grant writer starts with a first proposal. With the right techniques and determination, you can easily turn your nonprofit's vision into reality.

Grant funding is essential for not only the survival but also the growth of nonprofit organizations. Unlike for-profit entities, you rely significantly on external funding sources to support your programs, initiatives, and operations. Grants offer a large portion of this funding, allowing you to pursue your missions without the pressure of generating revenue through commercial sources.

One of the main benefits of grant funding is its capability to sustain areas of need or fund specific projects that align with your objectives. These funds can be utilized to launch new initiatives, expand your existing services, or address emerging community challenges; thereby enabling your organization to remain impactful and responsive. Additionally, grants often come with fewer restrictions than other funding sources, giving you the flexibility to innovate and implement creative solutions to social challenges.

Grants also enhance your visibility and credibility. Securing a grant from a government agency or reputable foundation acts as an endorsement of your organization's work, enhancing its legitimacy and attractiveness to other potential partners and funders. This, in turn, can create a ripple effect, opening doors to numerous funding opportunities and collaborations.

The grant proposal process is a structured approach that can transform your organization's vision into a compelling request for funding. This process consists of many key steps, each significant to crafting a successful proposal. Let us take a brief glimpse into this process.

First, you need to recognize potential funders whose priorities reflect your organization's mission and project goals. Conduct thorough research to secure a good match between your nonprofit and the funder's requirements and interests.

Second, understand the specific criteria and guidelines of the funding opportunity. This can consist of the required documents, application format, and deadlines. Each funder will have unique expectations, so attention to detail is vital.

The heart of the proposal includes several components: the executive summary, project description, budget, needs statement, and evaluation plan. The executive summary offers a snapshot of your proposal and underscores the most significant points. The needs statement usually explains the challenge or issue your project aims to address, supported by data and evidence. The project description highlights the objectives, tasks, and timeline of your initiative. The budget describes the financial requirements along with the allocation of resources. Ultimately, the evaluation plan details how you will measure the project's impact and success.

After drafting the proposal, you need to review and refine it to ensure coherence, persuasiveness, and clarity. You can also seek feedback from mentors or colleagues to strengthen this narrative.

Submitting the proposal on time is paramount, followed by maintaining effective communication with the funder. If awarded, you should adhere to reporting requirements and foster a good relationship for future opportunities.

This structured approach to the grant proposal process enhances your chances of securing the funding required to advance your nonprofit's mission and make a positive and lasting impact.

The most important step in crafting a proposal is providing a detailed description of the challenges that you want to address, the goals of your project, and the specific action you will undertake for this purpose. Also, clearly explain how you will measure your success along the way. This not only helps you tailor a persuasive proposal but also tells your funders that you have a well-thought-out approach and are fully equipped to deliver tangible outcomes.

Cultivating strong relationships with potential funders can significantly improve your chances of success. You should engage with your funders through preliminary inquiries, attend their informational sessions or events, and seek feedback on your ideas. Personal connections as well as an understanding of your funder's perspective will provide you with a set of valuable insights. This, in turn, will help you refine your proposal.

In addition, assembling a dedicated and capable team to support the grant-writing process is critical. This team should include people with strong writing skills, a profound understanding of your organization's initiatives or programs, as well as the ability to manage details and deadlines. Collaboration blended with clear communication within your team will ensure that every component of the proposal is cohesive and well-developed.

Ultimately, make sure that your proposal is error-free and meticulously prepared. Adhere strictly to your funder's guidelines, submission deadlines, and format requirements. A polished and professional proposal reflects the reliability and quality of your organization.

So, if you are a professional looking forward to further attaining tangible results, let *The Art of Grant Proposals: Winning Strategies for Nonprofit Success* be your roadmap to unlocking your organization's potential and creating a lasting impact in the communities you aim to serve. However, if you are interested in joining the nonprofit world, my other book *Impactful Giving* will help you grasp the fundamentals of fundraising, while *Empowering Nonprofit Boards* will offer you insights into effective governance.

Together, let us change your passion into powerful proposals that can win the support you need to embrace success.

So, let the journey commence!

Chapter 1:

Understanding Grant Opportunities

Navigating the world of grant opportunities can seem like unlocking a treasure chest full of potential. For you, it is not merely a lifeline of financial support but a validation of impactful projects as well as innovative ideas.

Each grant application aims to recount a story brimming with hope and ambition, woven with the promise of making a lasting difference. However, the path to securing these funds is sometimes fraught with competition and complexities.

Understanding how to effectively recognize, apply for, and manage grants can change your aspirations into accomplishments, opening gates to new possibilities and driving meaningful change in many fields.

Let us master the art of grant applications, as they can significantly amplify your project's impact and reach.

Researching and Identifying Relevant Grant Opportunities

Finding the best grant opportunities for your nonprofit is the first significant step in the grant proposal process. This entails identifying funders who are passionate about supporting the kind of work your organization does and confirming that their funding priorities align with your project goals and mission. Below is a guide to help you navigate this task.

Understand Your Needs and Goals

Before conducting thorough research, you need to clarify what you need funding for. Do you want to start a new program, grow an existing one, or cover general operating costs? Knowing your objectives will help you find the right funders. For instance, if you are running a youth mentoring program and need funds to expand your outreach, you will need to look for grants focused on youth education or development.

Start With Online Databases and Resources

Multiple online databases can help you explore grant opportunities. Here are just a few examples:

- **Grants.gov:** This is a complete resource for federal grants. For instance, if you are working on a community health initiative, you can aim to find grants from the Department of Health and Human Services.

- **Candid's Foundation Directory:** This tool offers thorough information on private foundations. If you are a nonprofit focused on environmental conservation, you can explore many private foundations, such as the Sierra Club Foundation, that can align with your mission. You can find it at the following web address: fconline.foundationcenter.org

Use Keywords Effectively

When you are searching databases, you will need to use specific keywords associated with your project. For example, if you are aiming to seek funding for an after-school arts program, you should try terms, such as "after-school programs," "youth arts funding," and "arts education."

Explore Local Resources

Explore local opportunities. Community foundations and local businesses sometimes offer grants to support local nonprofits. For instance, a local bank can offer you small grants for community development projects, or a regional foundation could help fund health and wellness programs in your region.

Network and Seek Recommendations

Ensure that you talk to other nonprofits and colleagues in your field. They may know of grant opportunities that are not usually widely advertised. For instance, if you are part of a network of food banks, you should ask others where they have successfully secured grants. Networking events, social media groups, and professional associations can also be helpful sources of information.

Review Funder Priorities and Past Grants

Once you have identified potential funders, dig deeper into their past grant recipients and priorities. Many foundations have websites where they regularly list their funding priorities, missions, and examples or testimonials of past grants. This research will help you decide if a funder is a good fit or not. For instance, if a foundation has regularly funded science, technology, engineering, and mathematics (STEM) education initiatives, they can be a good fit for your science education initiative.

Attend Grant Workshops and Webinars

Numerous foundations as well as grant-making organizations offer webinars and workshops to help applicants comprehend their funding priorities and process. These sessions can offer valuable insights and tips for creating a successful proposal. For example, you can attend a webinar hosted by the National Science Foundation if you are seeking funds for technology initiatives.

Keep Track and Stay Organized

As you research, develop a system to track your potential grant opportunities. You can utilize a spreadsheet to record main details such as required materials, contact information, and application deadlines. This organization will assist you in managing multiple applications and ensure you do not miss noteworthy deadlines.

Be Realistic and Selective

Although it is tempting to apply for every grant you find, it is more effective to merely focus on the opportunities that best align with your organization's capacity and mission. Applying for a grant that does not align well with your objectives or that demands resources you do not have can be a waste of both time and effort.

Let us use an example to help you understand.

Suppose you are running a nonprofit that provides technology education to underprivileged communities. You begin by using keywords such as "digital literacy funding," "technology education grants," and "STEM education grants" in the mentioned databases (Grants.gov and Candid's Foundation Directory). You succeed in finding a grant from a tech company's foundation that supports digital literacy programs for underserved communities. By revisiting their past grants, you notice that they have funded similar projects, signaling a good match.

Subsequently, you check your local resources and explore a community foundation offering grants for educational projects in your region. Networking at a local association meeting, you get to know about a lesser-known grant from a nearby university supporting community tech education initiatives. Eventually, you attend a webinar organized and hosted by the tech company's foundation to achieve insights into their application process.

By following these steps, you can identify and pursue the most suitable grant opportunities for your nonprofit, enhancing your chances of securing the funding you need to accomplish your mission.

Assessing Eligibility Criteria and Alignment With Organizational Goals

Once you have successfully identified your potential grant opportunities, the next vital step is to evaluate whether these grants are a suitable fit for your nonprofit. This encompasses carefully assessing the eligibility criteria of every grant and ensuring that they match your organizational goals. You can effectively perform this assessment by focusing on the steps below.

Understand the Funder's Requirements

Every grant opportunity will have some eligibility criteria that detail who can apply. These criteria can consist of

- **Type of organization:** Some grants are merely available to specific types of nonprofits, like 501(c)(3) organizations, faith-based groups, or educational institutions (Hoy, 2018).

- **Geographic focus:** Numerous funders restrict their grants to organizations that are operating within certain geographic areas, such as specific states, cities, or countries.

- **Field of interest:** Funders usually have specific areas they support, such as education, the environment, healthcare, or arts and culture.

Match With Your Organizational Goals

Assess how well the funder's priorities match with your nonprofit's goals and mission. This ensures that their grant will support projects that are central to the work of your organization.

- **Mission alignment:** Ensure that the potential funder's values and mission align with your organization's mission. A good match will increase the possibility of a successful partnership.

- **Project fit:** Determine if the specific program or project you are seeking funding for fits within the funder's priorities and interests.

Assess Your Capacity

Make sure that your organization can meet the grant requirements, both in terms of project execution and application preparation.

- **Application requirements:** Examine whether you have the resources to prepare a solid application, including proposal writing, budget preparation, and data collection.

- **Implementation capacity:** Ensure that you can deliver the project efficiently if funded. This consists of having the necessary staff, infrastructure, and expertise.

Consider Restrictions and Conditions

Review if there are any conditions or restrictions attached to the grant, like how funds can be used, compliance issues, or reporting requirements. For example, a grant that does not allow funds to be used for programmatic purposes might not be ideal if you need help with overhead costs.

Make a Go/No-Go Decision

Based on the information collected, decide if you want to pursue the grant. This decision needs to be a strategic one, balancing the potential advantages against the requirements of applying for and managing the grant. For instance, if a grant provides substantial funding for a project entirely aligned with your mission but demands complex reporting that can strain your resources, you should consider other options.

Practical Steps

1. **Create a checklist:** Craft a checklist of alignment factors and eligibility criteria for each potential grant.

2. **Hold a review meeting:** Ensure that you gather your team to review each grant opportunity, discussing how well it can fit with your organization's capacity and goals.

3. **Prioritize opportunities:** Consider ranking the grants based on their alignment with your ease of application and potential impact.

Building Relationships With Grantmakers and Funders

When you are aiming for the long-term success of your nonprofit, cultivating strong relationships with funders and grantmakers becomes a necessity. These relationships can help lead you to better funding opportunities, practical advice, and lasting partnerships. You can effectively cultivate these connections by implementing these strategies:

Do Your Homework

Before contacting potential funders, research their past grants, funding priorities, and interests. This demonstrates that you respect their time and efforts and are genuinely interested in a partnership. For example, if a foundation has a past of supporting after-school programs, you can mention how your youth mentoring program perfectly aligns with their focus when you first reach out to them.

Do an Introduction

Begin by introducing your organization and its goals. A concise but well-crafted introductory letter or email can help you make a great first impression. Emphasize how your work aligns with their passion and why you have faith in the potential for collaboration.

You can craft an introduction like this:

"Dear [Funder's Name], I am reaching out to you to introduce [Your Nonprofit], a nonprofit organization devoted to enhancing digital literacy among underprivileged youth. Given your foundation's dedication to education, we believe synergies exist between your mission and our work."

Attend Events and Workshops

Many grantmakers and foundations host workshops, webinars, or events. Attending these gatherings and events is an effective way to meet funders in person, learn more about their preferences and interests, and network with your fellow nonprofit leaders.

When you participate in a local community foundation's grant workshops, you use this opportunity to introduce yourself to the foundation's team. Moreover, ask thoughtful questions about their funding procedure.

Be Authentic and Transparent

Honesty is essential when building trust. Be clear and honest about your organization's goals, needs, and challenges. Funders will appreciate transparency and are more likely to support your organization if you are open and honest.

You can say, "We are now expanding our after-school STEM program and are needing additional funding to reach more students. Although we have a strong curriculum, we need resources for additional materials and staff."

Communicate Regularly

Even after you have received a grant, keep your funders updated on your progress. Regular updates illustrate that you value their support and are dedicated to maintaining a positive and lasting relationship. You can send quarterly newsletters outlining your nonprofit's accomplishments and the impact of the funder's support. Include statistics and stories that illustrate progress.

Invite Funders to Visit

Inviting funders to see your work and progress firsthand can be very impactful. A visit allows funders and grantmakers to see the direct effect of their support and cultivate a more profound connection with your organization.

You can invite them by saying, "We would love for you to come to our community center to witness our after-school program in action. It is a wonderful opportunity to meet the students and witness how your support is making a lasting difference."

Show Gratitude

Always show gratitude for any support you get. A sincere thank-you note, a public acknowledgment, or a mention in your annual report at an event can go a long way.

Seek Feedback

"We would really appreciate your feedback on our recent grant proposal. Your insights are invaluable as we aim to better align with your priorities and refine our programs."

Request feedback on your performance and proposals. This illustrates that you are committed to consistent improvement and value your funder's insights.

Foster Long-Term Relationships

Make it a habit to think beyond immediate funding needs. You should aim to cultivate lasting relationships that can further contribute to sustained collaboration and support over time. For instance, once you have completed a project funded by a grant, ensure you reach out to discuss future initiatives and think about ways to continue working together.

1. **Create a relationship map:** List your potential and current funders, highlighting key contacts, past interactions, and interests.

2. **Plan regular updates:** You can schedule regular updates and check-ins with your funders.

3. **Host events:** Organize or host open houses or events to showcase your work and thank your donors.

Chapter 2:

Crafting a Compelling Proposal Narrative

Did you know that more than 90% of startups fail within their first year due to a lack of a clear vision and planning? (Burnett-Thompson, 2020). This statistic shows the importance of creating a well-thought-out proposal narrative that can capture the imagination and convince your funders of the viability as well as potential success of a project.

In the world of nonprofits, where each idea competes for attention and investment, the proposal narrative acts as the backbone of any successful venture. It transforms a simple idea into an effective vision, highlighting not only the possibility for success but also the creative spirit behind the project.

Your proposal is not only a document; rather, it is a strategic roadmap tailored to inspire confidence and ignite enthusiasm. It is structured to address the main concerns and questions that your potential partners, investors, and funders might have. Through a thorough exploration of market opportunities, detailed financial projections, and competitive analysis, you will demonstrate the robustness of your plan and its alignment with wider industry trends.

Additionally, this proposal narrative is created with a focus on both sustainability and long-term growth. It summarizes innovative strategies that promise immediate impact and guarantees the project's relevance and adaptability in changing times. With the right vision, unwavering dedication, and strategic approach, you can change your proposal from simply a narrative to a groundbreaking reality.

In this chapter, we will learn how to craft a compelling narrative.

Developing the Project Description

A riveting proposal acts as the blueprint for your project, giving potential funders a comprehensive understanding of what you want to accomplish, how you plan to accomplish it, and why it matters.

Crafting an effective project description involves clearly articulating your goals, emphasizing your methods, and illustrating the anticipated impact. In the following sections, we will explore these components to guide you in creating a standout project description.

Articulating Clear Objectives

The first and foremost step in crafting a captivating project description is to articulate specific, clear, and measurable goals. These goals must align with your organization's mission and talk about a concrete need within your target community. They are the foundation upon which the rest of your project description will be built.

Let us say your nonprofit is dedicated to improving literacy rates among underserved children. A clear goal can be: "To enhance and improve reading proficiency among 300 elementary school students in [a specific community] by at least 2 grade levels within 2 academic years."

This goal is specific (targeting reading proficiency), measurable (improving by at least two grade levels), achievable (based on your organization's expertise and capacity), relevant (aligned with your organization's mission to improve literacy), and time-bound (within 2 academic years).

Outlining Your Methods

Once you have specified your goals or objectives, the next step is to outline the means you will utilize to acquire them. This section should offer a detailed plan of action, explaining the resources, activities, and timelines involved. It is very important to be as specific as possible, as this illustrates your organization's capacity and preparedness to execute the project.

Example

Continuing with your literacy project, your methods section should include

- **Activity 1: Establishing after-school reading programs**
    - Hire and train six qualified reading instructors by September.
    - Partner with local schools to recognize and recruit 300 students by October.
    - Conduct reading sessions three times a week for one hour, starting in November.
- **Activity 2: Providing access to learning materials**
    - Purchase age-appropriate books and reading materials by August.
    - Build a lending library to encourage students to take books home.
- **Activity 3: Engaging parents and guardians**
    - Schedule monthly workshops to prepare parents with the necessary skills to support their children's reading at home.
    - Distribute biweekly newsletters with resources and tips for reading activities and tasks.

Each of these activities must be followed by a timeline and a description of the resources needed, such as staff, funding, and materials. Moreover, you should illustrate how these activities will collectively contribute to the attainment of your goals.

Demonstrating Anticipated Impact

You will convince funders of the importance and value of your project in the impact section of your project description. This consists of explaining how your project will make a lasting difference in the lives of your target population or community and lead to broader societal objectives. Your potential funders want to know that their investment and time will contribute to making important and positive outcomes.

Example

For the literacy project, the impact should be

- **Immediate impact:** By the end of the first academic year, at least 85% of participating students will show an improvement in reading proficiency of one grade level or more, as calculated by standardized reading assessments.

- **Long-term impact:** Enhanced reading skills will improve students' overall academic performance, resulting in higher graduation rates and enhancing their future prospects for higher education and employment.

- **Broader societal impact:** Enhanced literacy rates in the community will lead to minimized poverty levels and improved economic development, as literacy is closely associated with individual and community prosperity.

To bolster your case, you can add data and evidence from similar programs, letters of support from donors or community leaders, or testimonials from beneficiaries. This will not only add credibility to your proposal but also demonstrate a well-rounded knowledge of the issue and the potential for your project to bring lasting and meaningful change.

Tips for Crafting Your Project Description

1. **Be concise and focused:** While it is important to be thorough, you should avoid overwhelming your reader with too much detail. You need to keep your descriptions focused on the main points.

2. **Use strong, active language:** Employing active language will make your proposal more persuasive and engaging. Rather than saying, "The program aims to make reading skills better," you can say, "The program will enhance reading skills."

3. **Incorporate visuals:** If appropriate or needed, use graphs, charts, or infographics to visually showcase your methods along with expected outcomes. This will make complex information more persuasive and accessible.

4. **Align with funder priorities:** Craft your project description to align with the interests and priorities of the funder. Outline how your project addresses their specific objectives and goals.

5. **Seek feedback:** Before submitting your proposal, you can seek feedback from external advisors, board members, or colleagues. They can give you valuable insights and help you work on areas for improvement.

Assessing Eligibility Criteria and Alignment With Organizational Goals

An important step in crafting a grant proposal is ensuring that your nonprofit is not only eligible for the funding opportunity but also that the proposed project perfectly aligns with your organization's objectives and the funder's criteria. This assessment will save time and resources and increase the likelihood of securing the grant. You can effectively assess eligibility criteria and ensure alignment with organizational goals by focusing on these points:

Understanding Eligibility Criteria

Eligibility criteria are the distinctive requirements that funders set to determine which organizations can apply for their grants. These criteria can vary, including factors such as geographic location, organizational size, type of services offered, and target population.

Imagine a nonprofit, Healthy Futures, which mainly focuses on offering health education and services to underserved communities. It is now considering applying for a grant from a foundation that supports such health initiatives. The foundation's eligibility criteria clarify that all applicants must be registered 501(c)(3) organizations, work within the state of California, and have an annual operating budget of less than $3 million.

Healthy Futures, a 501(c)(3) organization located in Los Angeles with an annual budget of $2.5 million, meets all these requirements. So, it is eligible to apply for this grant. However, understanding eligibility criteria is merely the first step.

Ensuring Alignment With Organizational Goals

While eligibility criteria may determine whether an organization can apply for funding, alignment with organizational objectives decides whether it should apply. This encompasses evaluating whether the funder's priorities as well as the specific grant objectives match your values, mission, and strategic goals.

Suppose, Healthy Futures' mission is to enhance health outcomes in underserved communities through education and preventive services. The grant it is looking for focuses on innovative health education initiatives for low-income families. This aligns well with the goals of Healthy Futures, as its strategic plan talks about expanding its health education outreach.

To evaluate alignment, Healthy Futures will focus on the following questions:

- **Mission compatibility:** Does this grant support activities and programs that further our mission?

- **Strategic fit:** Does this grant align with our current priorities and strategic goals?

- **Capacity:** Do we have the skill, talent, and resources to effectively implement this project if funded?

- **Sustainability:** Will this project have long-term advantages, and how will we successfully sustain it once the grant period ends?

Conducting a Thorough Assessment

To conduct a comprehensive assessment, you should create a systematic approach to evaluate potential grants. This can include

1. **Developing a grant readiness checklist:** A checklist should be able to quickly determine if a grant opportunity is worth pursuing or not. This should include basic eligibility criteria and initial questions about alignment with the organization's goals.

2. **Engaging key stakeholders:** Include your board members, staff, and possibly beneficiaries in discussions and meetings about potential grants to ensure a thorough understanding and buy-in.

3. **Reviewing past grant successes and failures:** Analyze your past grant applications and outcomes to recognize patterns and learn what kinds of projects have been most successful and why.

4. **Aligning with strategic plan:** Ensure that this grant project is a great fit with your organization's strategic plan and can be incorporated into other existing programs without causing major disruption.

Strategic Grant Management: A Framework for Success

1. **Create a decision-making framework:** Create a clear framework for assessing and evaluating grants that should include eligibility plus alignment criteria.

2. **Stay mission-focused:** Always resist and avoid the temptation to chase funding that demands significant deviations from not only your mission but also strategic goals.

3. **Build relationships with funders:** Engage with your potential funders to better understand their interests and priorities and cultivate long-term partnerships.

4. **Be honest about capacity:** Make sure that you have the skill to deliver on the grant's demands without compromising your existing programs.

5. **Use technology:** Use grant management software to track other opportunities, deadlines, and application progress.

By systematically assessing all these factors, you can focus your efforts on opportunities that not only offer the necessary funding but also contribute to advancing your mission and strategic goals. This strategic approach will increase the possibility of securing funding and ensure that your organization remains true to its primary purpose and delivers meaningful and sustainable impact.

Building Relationships With Grantmakers and Funders

Cultivating and fostering relationships with grantmakers is an ongoing process that demands communication, effort, and a focus on mutual goals. When you understand funder priorities, initiate meaningful contact, communicate effectively, demonstrate impact, and show appreciation, you start building strong and lasting relationships that breed sustained support and collaboration. These relationships are not merely about securing funding; instead, they are about cultivating honest partnerships that advance your mission and create lasting and positive change.

Understanding the Significance of Relationships

Solid relationships with funders are based on mutual respect, clear communication, and trust. These relationships have several benefits:

1. **Insight into funder priorities:** By comprehending your funder's priorities, you can design your proposals to better align with their interests.

2. **Constructive feedback:** Funders can offer valuable feedback on your proposals, enhancing the possibility of future success.

3. **Ongoing support:** A strong relationship can contribute to long-term partnerships, with funders offering ongoing financial support and resources.

4. **Networking opportunities:** Funders can also introduce you to other potential partners, stakeholders, and donors.

Steps to Build Strong Relationships

1. **Research and understand funders:**

    - **Identify potential funders:** Use networks, databases, and research to recognize funders whose missions match your organization's objectives.

    - **Learn about their priorities:** Study their mission statements, funding history, and any published reports or guidelines to understand their interests and priorities.

2. **Initiate contact:**
   - **Introduce your organization:** Send a short and well-crafted introduction letter or email that outlines your mission, impact, and why you believe there is a strong alignment with the funder's interests.
   - **Request a meeting:** Whenever possible, you can request a meeting (in-person or virtual) to discuss potential collaboration as well as learn more about your funder's priorities.

3. **Communicate effectively:**
   - **Be clear and concise:** When communicating with your funders, be concise, clear, and to the point. Avoid jargon and make sure that your messages are easy to comprehend.
   - **Listen actively:** During meetings, you need to listen carefully to the funder's insights and feedback. Show authentic interest in their concerns.

4. **Demonstrate impact:**
   - **Share success stories:** Periodically update funders on your organization's progress.
   - **Provide transparency:** Be transparent about your challenges and successes. Honesty cultivates trust and shows that your organization is accountable and reliable.

5. **Show appreciation:**
   - **Thank funders promptly:** Always thank your funders promptly for their support. Also, acknowledge their contributions.
   - **Highlight their Impact:** Show your funders how their support is making a difference in the lives you are

serving. Personalized reports along with stories that link their funding to solid outcomes can be very effective.

Tips for Sustaining Relationships

1. **Consistency is key:** Maintain regular communication with your funders. Regular updates and check-ins can help keep your organization top-of-mind.

2. **Be proactive:** Do not wait for funders to reach out. Instead, you should proactively share news, progress, successes, and updates.

3. **Adapt to feedback:** Show your funders that you value their input by integrating their feedback into your proposals and programs.

4. **Celebrate milestones together:** Invite your funders to celebrate each milestone and achievement. This reinforces their role in your success and establishes a strong sense of partnership.

Chapter 3:

Budgeting and Financial Planning

Writing a winning grant proposal is undoubtedly a form of art, one that can significantly impact the success of your organization. According to the National Center for Charitable Statistics, there are more than 1.8 million nonprofit organizations registered in the United States (Candid Learning, n.d.). With such a large number of organizations vying for funding, competition has become fierce. To stand out, your grant proposal must be enthralling, meticulously planned, and financially sound.

A survey by the Grant Professionals Association disclosed that more than half of grant applications are rejected not only due to poor budgeting but also financial planning (Grant, 2024). This statistic highlights the crucial role of strategic and accurate financial planning in securing grant funding.

In the realm of grant writing, a well-crafted budget is not just numbers on a page; it is a financial illustration that tells potential funders a story of accountability, sustainability, and impact. It showcases your organization's skill to effectively manage resources and attain its mission. If you excel in financial planning, you are also more likely to gain the trust of funders, as you exhibit foresight and transparency.

This chapter delves deeper into the main strategies and best practices for budgeting as well as financial planning, providing you with the necessary tools you need to create compelling and fund-worthy grant proposals.

Creating a Realistic and Comprehensive Project Budget

A well-crafted budget not only highlights the financial goals and needs of the project but also demonstrates your organization's capability to manage funds effectively. This further cultivates confidence among potential funders, multiplying the chances of securing the required financial support.

The Importance of a Comprehensive Budget

A comprehensive project budget offers a detailed breakdown of all anticipated costs linked with the project. This consists of direct costs, like equipment, materials, and salaries, as well as indirect costs, such as facility maintenance and administrative support. By accounting for every expense, the budget guarantees that there are no surprises down the line and that your project can be achieved as planned.

Steps to Creating a Realistic Budget

Define the Project Scope

Before you create a budget, you should have a clear understanding of your project's scope. This encompasses defining the goals, activities, and results of the project. For instance, if a nonprofit organization plans to launch a community health initiative, the scope will include conducting health screenings, follow-up consultations, and educational workshops.

Identify and Categorize Costs

Once your project scope has been defined, the next step is to highlight all the costs linked to each component of the project. These costs can be classified into direct and indirect costs:

- **Direct costs:** These are costs that are directly attributable to your project activities. Examples are
    - **Personnel:** This includes salaries and wages for staff involved in the project. For example, if the health initiative needs to hire nurses, health educators, and a project manager, their salaries will be direct costs.
    - **Supplies and equipment:** These are costs for tools and materials required for the project, such as medical supplies for health screenings and educational materials for workshops.
    - **Travel:** Expenses for lodging, meals, and transportation if your project staff needs to travel should be included.
    - **Consultants and contractors:** These are fees for service providers or external experts. If the initiative demands specialized health professionals or training facilitators, their fees would be considered as a direct cost.
- **Indirect costs:** These are overhead costs that do not directly tie to the project but are essential for its implementation. Examples include
    - **Administrative support:** This is a proportionate share of the earnings or salaries of administrative staff.
    - **Facility costs:** This includes rent, maintenance, and utilities for the facilities utilized for the project.
    - **General office supplies:** These are costs for office supplies and communication tools.

Research and Estimate Costs

Accurate cost estimation is essential for a realistic budget. This comprises researching current market rates for services and goods. For instance, if your project demands purchasing medical supplies, your organization should obtain quotes from numerous suppliers to get an accurate estimate. Likewise, salary rates need to be based on existing industry standards.

Allocate Resources

With costs specified and estimated, the next step is to allocate resources efficiently. This consists of assigning a specific sum of money to each budget category. It is vital to be as precise as possible and include justifications for each expense. For example, if your budget has a line item for health educators, your proposal should explain how many educators are needed, the duration of their involvement, and their roles.

Include a Contingency Plan

Unexpected costs can surface during the project's implementation. To mitigate this, it is prudent to have a contingency fund in the budget, typically around 5%–10% of the total project cost (Patil, 2024). This helps guarantee that your project can continue seamlessly even if unforeseen expenses occur.

Review and Revise

Once you have drafted your initial budget, you should review it carefully. This includes ensuring mathematical accuracy, checking that all costs are justified, as well as confirming that your budget perfectly aligns with your project's goals and activities. It is also beneficial to have a third party, like a financial expert or board member, review the budget for any errors and overlooked items.

Example of a Project Budget

To further explain, let us consider a hypothetical nonprofit organization, Healthy Communities Initiative, planning a one-year community health project. Below is a simplified version of their project budget.

Direct Costs

- **Personnel:**
    - Project manager: $40,000
    - Health educators (4 at $40,000 each): $160,000
- **Supplies and equipment:**
    - Medical supplies: $30,000
    - Educational materials: $20,000
- **Travel:**
    - Local travel for health educators: $8,000
- **Consultants and Contractors:**
    - Nutrition specialist: $20,000

Indirect Costs

- **Administrative support:**
  - Administrative assistant (portion of salary): $15,000
- **Facility costs:**
  - Office rent and utilities: $18,000
- **General office supplies:**
  - Office supplies and communication: $4,000
- **Contingency fund:**
  - 5% of total direct and indirect costs: $15,750

Total Project Budget: $330,750

Best Tips for Budget Presentation

A well-constructed budget can significantly increase the credibility of a grant proposal:

- **Clarity and detail:** Pay extra attention to make sure that the budget is detailed as well as clear, with each expense justified and itemized.
- **Consistency:** The budget needs to be consistent with the narrative of your proposal. Any discrepancies between the project description and budget can give birth to red flags for funders.
- **Visual aids:** Using charts and tables can help you present your budget in an easily understandable format.
- **Transparency:** Again, be transparent and clear about how costs were calculated and give proper justifications for each expense.

Justifying Budget Items and Expenses

Justifying budget items and expenses is an important aspect of crafting a compelling grant proposal for your organization. Funders want to see that their money will be used efficiently and effectively to attain the proposed project's objectives. Justification consists of giving clear and detailed explanations for each budget line item, illustrating how each expense leads to the project's success.

A well-justified budget shows that your organization has planned the project in detail, understands the expenses involved, and is committed to accountability and responsibility. Justification offers rationale and context, transforming the budget from a list of expenses into a narrative that details the impact and necessity of each expenditure.

Understanding the Importance of Justification

When you are justifying budget items, it is important to think from the perspective of the funder. Your well-justified budget should mainly answer these questions:

- Why is this expense required?
- How was the cost specified?
- What impact will this expense have on accomplishing our project goals?

Steps to Justify Budget Items

Step 1: Link Expenses to Project Objectives

Each budget item needs to be directly linked to the project's activities and objectives. For example, if a nonprofit is offering a community literacy program, expenses can include costs for hiring educators, renting space for classes, and purchasing books. Justifying these expenses will involve explaining how each cost supports the project's objectives. For instance:

- **Educators:** "Hiring qualified literacy educators is important to deliver high-quality instruction to participants, ensuring they attain notable improvements in reading and writing skills."

- **Books and materials:** "Purchasing age-appropriate and diverse reading materials will cater to the varied needs of participants, cultivating a love for reading and improving literacy outcomes."

- **Facility rental:** "Renting a community center offers a safe and accessible space for classes, promoting consistent attendance and participation."

Step 2: Provide Detailed Cost Estimates

Detailed cost estimates illustrate that your organization has researched and accurately anticipated costs. This includes offering quotes or market rates for goods and services. Every budget item needs to have a detailed and clear description explaining what it is, why it is important, and how the cost was determined. You should avoid vague terms and be specific. For example, if you are requesting funds for personnel, you need to specify each staff member's responsibilities, roles, and time commitment.

Rather than listing "staff salaries" as a line item, you need to break it down as follows:

- **Project manager (full-time, 12 months):**
    - $50,000
    - Accountable for managing staff, overall project coordination, and ensuring project milestones are achieved.

- **Health educators (3 positions, full-time, 12 months):**
  - $120,000
  - Conduct educational workshops, health screenings, and follow-up consultations.

Step 3: Explain the Necessity of Each Item

Justification should contain explanations of why each expense is required for your project's success. For instance:

- **Nutrition specialist (consultant, 12 months):**
  - $15,000
  - The nutrition specialist will develop customized nutrition plans for participants, conduct workshops on healthy eating, and deliver individual consultations. This role is critical for addressing the dietary element of the health initiative.

Step 4: Use Data and Research

You should support your budget items with data and research to justify costs. This can consist of salary surveys, market rates, historical cost data from similar projects, or price quotes from suppliers.

Example: If you are going to include travel expenses, you should provide a detailed breakdown:

- **Local travel for health educators:**
  - $5,785
  - Based on IRS standard mileage rates ($0.65 per mile) and estimated travel distance (almost 8,900 miles per year) for outreach activities.

Step 5: Demonstrate Cost-Effectiveness

Showing that your organization is using funds wisely is vital. This involves explaining cost-effectiveness through alternative options or comparisons. For instance:

- **In-kind contributions:** "We have secured in-kind donations of not only office space but also utilities, significantly minimizing overhead costs and enabling more funds to be directed to program initiatives."

- **Bulk purchasing:** "Purchasing materials in bulk from a wholesale supplier will minimize costs by 20% compared to retail prices, enabling us to serve more participants within the exact budget."

Best Practices for Effective Justification

1. **Consistency:** Ensure that your budget justification is consistent with your project narrative. Any discrepancies can contribute to undermining the credibility of your proposal.

2. **Clarity:** Avoid both jargon and overly technical language. The justification needs to be clear and understandable to someone who may not have complete knowledge of the field.

3. **Evidence-based:** Use quotes, past project experiences, and data to support your budget items.

4. **Proportionality:** Make sure that the scale of the budget is proportional to the duration and scope of your project. Insufficient or excessive budget requests can be seen as red flags by funders.

5. **Review and revise:** Have multiple stakeholders review your budget justification to catch any omissions or errors and to ensure it aligns with your overall project plan.

Demonstrating Financial Sustainability and Accountability

Demonstrating financial sustainability and accountability is a crucial element of a successful grant proposal. Funders not only want to ensure that their investments will be managed responsibly but also that the projects or initiatives they support will continue to operate even after the first funding period ends.

Financial sustainability is the capability of a nonprofit organization to maintain its operations and attain its mission over the long term. Financial accountability, on the other hand, involves ethical, transparent, and efficient management of funds. Let us take a look at a comprehensive guide on how to illustrate both in your winning grant proposal.

Financial Sustainability

Financial sustainability refers to demonstrating that your organization has a strong plan to secure ongoing funding and manage resources effectively. You can achieve this by implementing the following strategies.

Diversified Funding Sources

Most of the time, funders prefer to support organizations that do not depend on a single source of income. Show that your nonprofit has diversified funding sources, including but not limited to donations, fundraising events, grants, and earned income.

You can state: "Our nonprofit has a diversified funding portfolio including individual donations (30%), government grants (25%), corporate sponsorships (30%), and revenue from service fees and investments (15%). This diverse mix guarantees that we do not overly rely on any single funding base; thereby, boosting our financial stability."

Long-Term Financial Planning

Give evidence of long-term financial planning, such as financial forecasts, strategic plans, and multi-year budgets. This indicates to funders that your organization is proactive when it comes to planning for the future and handling its finances sustainably.

Example: "We have designed a five-year financial plan that includes a reserve fund strategy along with projected income and expenses. This plan is reviewed and updated every year to adapt to varying circumstances and ensure long-term sustainability."

Reserve Funds

Having an endowment or a reserve fund can illustrate financial prudence and sustainability. It indicates that your organization has savings to cover revenue shortfalls or unexpected expenses.

Example: "Our organization holds a reserve fund equivalent to eight months of operating expenses. This fund serves as a financial safety net, making sure that we can continue our programs and initiatives without disruption in case of unexpected funding gaps."

Future Funding Strategies

Highlight your strategies for securing future funding. This should include plans for enhancing donor engagement, developing partnerships with other organizations, and launching new fundraising campaigns.

Example: "We aim to launch a major donor campaign next year to enhance individual donations. Also, we are exploring partnerships with many local businesses to secure ongoing sponsorships and have several new grant opportunities that perfectly align with our mission."

Financial Accountability

Financial accountability entails demonstrating that your organization can manage its finances ethically, transparently, and efficiently. Below are essential components to highlight.

Transparent Financial Reporting

Demonstrate that your organization practices transparent financial reporting by delivering regular financial statements, audits, and annual reports. This transparency reassures your funders that you can manage their contributions responsibly.

Example: "We typically publish quarterly financial statements and an annual report on our website. Additionally, our financial records are audited annually by an independent accounting firm, ensuring full accountability and transparency."

Strong Internal Controls

You should describe the internal controls your organization has in place to avoid fraud and ensure the correct usage of funds. This consists of policies and procedures for financial management, such as regular financial reviews, approval processes for costs, and segregation of duties.

Example: "Our internal control system has segregated duties for handling cash, a strict approval procedure for expenditures, and regular reconciliation of bank statements. In addition to this, all financial transactions are reviewed by our finance committee each month."

Budget Monitoring and Evaluation

Provide details on how your organization monitors and assesses its budget to ensure funds are used as intended. Regular budget reviews and financial performance assessments show your commitment to responsible financial management.

Example: "We conduct budget reviews each month to compare actual costs against projections. This enables us to identify any changes early and adjust our spending accordingly. Additionally, our finance committee reviews these reports and offers oversight to ensure financial discipline."

Ethical Fund Management

Outline your organization's commitment to ethical fund management, such as adherence to ethical fundraising techniques and compliance with legal and regulatory requirements.

Example: "We adhere to the Ethical Standards for Fundraising Professionals, making sure that all our fundraising tasks are conducted with transparency and integrity. Moreover, we comply with all relevant laws and regulations, including those associated with nonprofit financial management."

Integrating Sustainability and Accountability in Your Grant Proposal

When you are incorporating financial sustainability and accountability into your grant proposal, it is of prime importance to weave these elements throughout the whole narrative. Here are some useful tips:

1. **Executive summary:** Briefly mention your organization's dedication and commitment to financial accountability and sustainability, setting a positive tone from the very start.

2. **Organizational background:** Include a section that explains your financial history, outlining past successes in securing and managing funds.

3. **Project budget:** Offer a detailed budget with justifications for each line item, illustrating careful planning and responsible financial management.

4. **Sustainability plan:** Include a dedicated section outlining your techniques for ensuring the long-term sustainability of your project and the organization.

5. **Financial controls:** Describe your financial monitoring processes, ethical fund management practices, and internal controls.

Chapter 4:
Demonstrating Organizational Capacity and Effectiveness

In the competitive world of grant funding, having a compelling project idea is not enough. Funders need assurance that your organization has the skills and effectiveness to turn their visions into reality. Demonstrating organizational capacity and effectiveness is very important in building this confidence. It showcases your ability to execute projects, achieve meaningful outcomes, and manage resources efficiently.

According to a survey, many grant applications fail not because of poor project ideas, but because of doubts about the applicant's ability to deliver on their promises on time (Tetlow, 2024). This makes it imperative for you to emphasize your strengths in governance, infrastructure, past performance, and staffing.

Organizational capacity is the collective ability of your nonprofit to carry out its mission effectively. This consists of having a solid governance structure, talented staff, efficient systems, and enough facilities. It is about showcasing that your organization is well-equipped to handle the administrative, technical, and logistical demands of the proposed project. Effectiveness, on the contrary, is about demonstrating your past accomplishments and the impact of your work. It is mainly about presenting stories and data that prove your initiatives or projects have made a real, lasting difference in the communities you serve.

In this chapter, we will delve into the main components of demonstrating organizational capacity and effectiveness, offering practical strategies to help your nonprofit stand out in the competitive landscape of grant applications.

Highlighting the Organization's Track Record and Accomplishments

Highlighting your organization's track record and achievements is a significant strategy in grant writing that details your ability to accomplish results and manage projects effectively. This fosters credibility with funders and significantly enhances the possibility of securing grants. Let us take a comprehensive look at how to effectively outline your organization's track record along with accomplishments.

Understanding the Importance

As funders invest in organizations they believe can keep up their promises, a solid track record can help you provide evidence of your nonprofit's reliability and capability. It reassures them that you have successfully managed similar projects in the past, attained significant results, and made a positive impact on the community.

Mission Alignment

Start by explaining how your past initiatives align with your organization's goals and mission. This illustrates that your work is consistent and focused on your key goals.

Example: "Our mission is to improve health outcomes in underserved communities. Over the past six years, we have launched many initiatives that align with this objective, including free medical check-ups, nutrition programs, and health education workshops."

Quantifiable Outcomes

Present clear and quantifiable data to demonstrate the impact of your previous projects. Your funders are interested in solid outcomes, such as improvements in primary indicators, cost savings attained, and the number of people served.

Example: "In our recent community health project, we offered health screenings to over 2,500 people, resulting in a 20% enhancement in early detection of chronic illnesses. Moreover, our nutrition workshops helped 600 families adopt healthier eating habits, leading to a 15% reduction in obesity rates within 2 years."

Success Stories and Testimonials

Including success stories and testimonials from beneficiaries adds a personal touch to your narrative. These stories offer compelling evidence of your impact and help them connect emotionally with your work.

Example: "Nadia, a participant in our health education program, recently shared a powerful testimonial about her experience. She explained that the workshops provided her with essential knowledge about the importance of regular health check-ups. This newfound understanding led her to schedule a routine examination, during which her diabetes was detected early. Thanks to this early intervention, Nadia was able to start treatment promptly, which has significantly improved her quality of life. She now manages her condition effectively and feels more empowered to take control of her health. Her story underscores the vital impact of our program on individuals in underserved communities."

Awards and Recognition

Highlight any recognitions, endorsements, or awards your organization has received. These accolades act as third-party validation of your credibility and effectiveness.

Example: "Our organization received the Community Impact Award from the Local Health Foundation in recognition of our health programs and significant contributions to enhancing public health. This prestigious award reflects our dedication to improving the well-being of underserved communities and highlights the positive impact of our initiatives. Moreover, we have been endorsed by many prominent health organizations and have received accolades, such as the Excellence in Health Education Award and the Public Health Innovation Award, further affirming our dedication and commitment to excellence as well as effectiveness in the field."

Partnerships and Collaborations

Showcase your collaborations and partnerships with other reputable organizations. This demonstrates your ability to work effectively within the community and leverage additional resources.

Example: "We have also partnered with schools, local hospitals, and community centers to expand the reach of our health projects. These partnerships have allowed us to deliver comprehensive services and support to a broader audience."

Financial Stewardship

Discuss your ability to manage funds responsibly. Discuss your ability to effectively utilize past grants to achieve your project objectives and maintain financial stability.

Example: "With the $60,000 grant received last year, we successfully launched a mobile health clinic serving over 4,000 individuals in remote areas. Our meticulous budgeting along with financial management ensured that every dollar was utilized effectively to amplify impact."

Structuring Your Accomplishments

When you are presenting your track record and achievements in a grant proposal, you should structure your information logically and clearly. You can use the format below.

Introduction

Begin with a brief introduction that sets the stage for your victories. Give a high-level overview of your organization's mission and the scope of your work.

Example: "Since our founding in 2009, our initiative has been dedicated to enhancing health outcomes in underserved communities through outreach, education, and direct services. This holistic approach addresses both immediate healthcare conditions and long-term well-being."

Major Accomplishments

Highlight your major accomplishments, especially focusing on those most relevant to the project. Use numbered lists or bullet points for clarity.

Example: "We accomplished the following:

- executed a community health education program that reached over 6,000 individuals, resulting in a 25% increase in health literacy
- launched a mobile health clinic that offered essential medical services to 4,000 people in remote areas
- partnered with local schools to initiate a nutrition education program, minimizing childhood obesity rates by 15% in participating schools"

Impact Metrics

Present detailed impact metrics to quantify your success. Use graphs or charts if applicable to represent your data visually.

Example: "In the past year, these initiatives have led to a:

- 15% increase in early detection of chronic conditions through health screenings,
- 20% increase in community participation in health education programs, and
- 35% improvement in patient follow-up rates at local health centers."

Success Stories and Testimonials

Again, include a few brief testimonials or success stories from beneficiaries to personalize your impact. Make sure that these stories are relevant and concise.

Financial Stewardship

Summarize your financial stewardship practices and outline any successful management of your last grants.

Example: "Our organization prides itself on effective and stringent financial management. Last year, we successfully managed a $60,000 grant from the Community Foundation, achieving all project milestones within budget and on time. Our financial audits consistently receive clean reports, reflecting our commitment to both accountability and transparency."

When you are concluding this section, you can reiterate how your track record and victories make your organization an effective and reliable partner for the proposed project.

You can say, "Our proven track record of impactful health projects, combined with our robust partnerships and solid financial management, positions us well to successfully implement and sustain the proposed project. We are dedicated to continuing our mission of enhancing community health and are confident that with your support, we can attain even greater results."

Showcasing Organizational Capacity and Capabilities

Organizational capacity and capabilities are required to effectively manage your resources, implement strategies, and achieve your mission and goals. These concepts can affect the efficiency, sustainability, and impact of your organization.

Organizational Capacity

Organizational capacity encompasses several elements that collectively enable your nonprofit to function effectively. It consists of human resources, infrastructure, financial resources, and intangible assets, such as relationships and reputation.

Human Resources

Human resources pertain to the volunteers, board members, and staff who contribute to the nonprofit's operations. Their expertise, commitment, and experience are important for carrying out your organization's mission. Cultivating capacity in this region involves training, recruiting, and retaining competent personnel, resulting in a positive organizational culture, and ensuring effective governance and leadership.

Infrastructure

Infrastructure refers to the technological and physical resources required for you to operate. This encompasses equipment, technology, office space, software systems, and computers. Robust infrastructure supports efficient operations and enhances your organization's ability to achieve its goals.

Financial Resources

Financial resources are essential to your capacity. This comprises funding from donations, grants, and other revenue-generating tasks. Effective financial management ensures that all resources are allocated correctly, expenses are controlled at all times, and the organization remains financially viable. It also consists of financial planning, budgeting, and maintaining transparency with your stakeholders.

Intangible Assets

Intangible assets, such as credibility, reputation, and relationships with stakeholders, also form a crucial part of your organizational capacity. A strong reputation can easily double the trust and support of your volunteers, beneficiaries, and donors. Effective communication and relationship management strategies are necessary for maintaining these intangible assets.

Organizational Capabilities

While capacity refers to the resources an organization has, capabilities are about how effectively these resources are utilized. They reflect the organization's competencies in executing its mission and achieving its objectives.

Strategic Planning

Strategic planning is a fundamental capability that consists of setting long-term objectives and determining the best means to embrace them. It requires a deep understanding of your organization's vision, mission, and values, as well as a clear analysis of the internal resources and external environment. Strategic planning can help you to prioritize your initiatives, distribute resources, and measure progress toward your goals.

Program Development and Implementation

You must be adept at creating and implementing programs that align with your mission. This capability should consist of program design, assessment, execution, monitoring, and evaluation to make sure that all your programs are effective and meet the needs of your target population or community. It also requires the skill to adapt and innovate in response to changing times.

Fundraising and Resource Mobilization

Effective fundraising and resource mobilization are other capabilities for sustaining your operations. This includes building diverse funding streams and relationships with funders and donors, including crafting compelling cases for support. You must master the art of grant writing, organizing and hosting fundraising events, as well as leveraging digital platforms and social media to attract and engage a wide range of supporters.

Advocacy and Public Policy

You can also engage in advocacy and public policy efforts to inform social change and advance your mission. This capability involves comprehending the policy landscape, building coalitions, and effectively communicating with both the public and policymakers. Advocacy requires persuasive communication, strategic thinking, and the ability to mobilize supporters.

Organizational Learning and Innovation

Organizational learning and innovation can guarantee continuous improvement and long-term success. This involves fostering a culture of learning, where feedback is appreciated, and mistakes and errors are seen as opportunities for growth. It also involves staying abreast of all industry trends, adopting effective practices, and experimenting with innovative approaches to address challenges and seize opportunities.

Enhancing Capacity and Capabilities

To enhance your organizational capacity and capabilities, you can invest in your staff development, strategic processes, and infrastructure. This can involve

- **Capacity building initiatives:** Initiatives and projects designed to strengthen your organizational capacity, such as training for board members and staff, investing in technology, and enhancing financial management systems.

- **Leadership development:** Cultivating the skills and capabilities of current and aspiring future leaders through mentorship, succession planning, and training.

- **Strategic alliances:** Forming partnerships and alliances with other organizations to share knowledge, expertise, and resources.

- **Performance measurement:** Implementing systems to measure and assess your organizational performance, including the efficiency of operations and the effectiveness of programs.

Providing Evidence of Past Success and Impact

We have frequently emphasized that providing evidence of your past success and impact is vital for you as it builds credibility, fosters trust with stakeholders, and demonstrates the effectiveness of your programs and initiatives. This evidence can take many forms, ranging from quantitative data and qualitative testimonials to documented results.

Importance of Evidence of Past Success

1. **Building credibility and trust:** Evidence of past success reassures funders, partners, and donors that your organization is reliable and capable. It shows that you have a track record of achieving your goals and making a lasting difference.

2. **Attracting funding and support:** Funders and donors will be more interested in investing in your organizations if you can demonstrate tangible results. Evidence of past success becomes a persuasive tool in not only grant applications but also fundraising campaigns.

3. **Demonstrating accountability and transparency:** Providing honest and transparent accounts of your past achievements mirrors your organization's commitment to accountability and transparency, which are essential traits for maintaining stakeholder trust.

4. **Encouraging continuous improvement:** By assessing and presenting past successes, you can determine what works well, facilitating continuous improvement and better programs in the future.

Types of Evidence

1. **Quantitative data:** Numerical data illustrates the scale and scope of your organization's impact. For example, a nonprofit committed to literacy can present data showing that they have distributed over 15,000 books to underserved communities and conducted 600 literacy workshops over the last year. They could also show that these efforts resulted in a 35% growth in reading levels among participating children. Simply put, this

data highlights the scale of your efforts and measurable impact on literary rates.

2. **Qualitative testimonials:** Personal stories and testimonials offer a human perspective on your work. They also add an emotional touch. For instance, an organization dedicated to working on mental health can include testimonials from multiple beneficiaries. A testimonial can read, "Before joining the counseling program, I dealt with extreme anxiety. After eight months of regular sessions, I have learned coping strategies that have largely enhanced my daily life."

3. **Documented outcomes:** Detailed reports and case studies that highlight specific accomplishments and their broader impact. For example, a nonprofit working on clean water can produce a very detailed case study of a village where they installed a new water purification system. The report can include that since the time of installation, there has been a 45% reduction in water diseases, enhanced school attendance, and a revived local economy due to fewer sick days. This case study offers a comprehensive view of the tangible impact, demonstrating how some interventions contribute to broader economic and social benefits.

How to Present Evidence

1. **Annual reports:** These documents can help you summarize the year's achievements with stories, visuals, and data.

2. **Impact reports:** These are focused reports that dive deeply into specific projects or programs, showcasing detailed testimonials and outcomes.

3. **Infographics and dashboards:** They are visual representations of data and outcomes that make information easily shareable and digestible.

4. **Presentations and pitches:** These are tailored presentations for stakeholders, funders, and the public that outline the main successes and impacts.

Chapter 5:

Addressing Evaluation and Impact Measurement

In today's competitive landscape, nonprofits are tasked with demonstrating their impact to funders, stakeholders, and the communities they serve. While some organizations successfully demonstrate their impact, others struggle and face negative consequences. To prevent such challenges, it's crucial to understand how to handle evaluation and impact measurement effectively.

But, before that, why should you measure your impact?

There are several reasons, such as that it helps you stay on track with your mission and goal. It also enhances the credibility and integrity of your organization. Most importantly, "impact evidence creates value" (Sheth, 2022).

Evaluation and impact measurement are not merely administrative tasks; they are vital for sustaining trust, securing funding and grants, and driving mission fulfillment. By systematically evaluating your programs, you can gain valuable insights into many areas, such as what works for you, work on areas for improvement, and make data-driven informed decisions. In addition, transparent reporting of impact ensures accountability and fosters stronger relationships with stakeholders.

This chapter delves deeper into the significance of assessment and impact measurement in the nonprofit sector. We will explore the main underpinnings of evaluation, discuss practical methods, and outline real-world examples of organizations that have successfully implemented comprehensive impact measurement systems.

Developing a Robust Evaluation Plan to Measure Project Outcomes

An evaluation plan is crucial for effectively measuring project results, demonstrating the impact of your work, and ensuring continual improvement. Such a plan can help your organization systematically collect, analyze, and use data to make more informed decisions.

Defining Clear Objectives and Goals

The basis of any evaluation plan is having a clear understanding of the project's objectives and goals. These should be Specific, Measurable, Achievable, Relevant, and Time-bound (SMART). For instance, a nonprofit committed to education may aim to enhance literacy rates among children in a specific community by 25% over 3 years. Clear goals offer a roadmap for what the evaluation aims to measure and help align your stakeholders on what success looks like.

Identifying Key Performance Indicators

Once the goals are set, the next important step is to identify key performance indicators (KPIs) that will successfully measure progress toward these objectives. KPIs need to be directly associated with the project's objectives. For instance, in the education example, relevant KPIs should include the number of children participating in the literacy program, their reading scores before and after the program, and school attendance rates. These indicators offer quantifiable data to help you evaluate the project's effectiveness.

Choosing the Right Evaluation Methods

Choosing appropriate evaluation methods is essential for gathering accurate and relevant data. Common methods are

- **Surveys and questionnaires:** Useful for gathering data from numerous participants about their experiences and outcomes.

- **Interviews and focus groups:** Give in-depth insights into participants' opinions and can unveil qualitative data that surveys might miss.

- **Observations:** Allow for direct assessment of program tasks and participant behaviors.

- **Administrative data analysis:** Utilizes existing data records, like performance records or attendance logs, to keep track of progress.

Using a mixed-methods approach can provide a more comprehensive understanding of the project's impact.

Developing Data Collection Tools

Effective data collection needs well-designed tools tailored to the chosen methods. This includes creating transparent, structured interview guides, unbiased survey questions, and customized observation checklists. Pilot testing these tools can help you identify and address any challenges before full implementation.

Establishing a Data Collection Timeline

A comprehensive data collection timeline ensures that the process is both systematic and manageable. This timeline should highlight when and how often data will be gathered, who will be responsible, and what resources are required. For instance, pre-program surveys can be conducted at the school year's beginning, with follow-up evaluations at mid-year and end-year to track progress.

Ensuring Data Quality and Integrity

Maintaining data quality and integrity is important when it comes to ensuring reliable evaluation outcomes. This consists of training data collectors, setting protocols for data entry and storage, as well as implementing measures to reduce errors and bias. Regular audits and consistency checks can help you ensure data accuracy.

Analyzing and Interpreting Data

Data analysis refers to converting raw data into meaningful and invaluable insights. Quantitative data can be analyzed utilizing statistical methods to identify trends and measure changes over time. Qualitative data analysis, on the contrary, involves thematic and coding analysis to extract noteworthy patterns and narratives. It is crucial to compare the findings against the set KPIs to assess whether the project is meeting its goals.

Reporting Findings

Straightforward, clear, and comprehensive reporting of findings is essential for accountability and transparency. Evaluation reports must present data in an accessible format, using graphs, narrative summaries, and charts to emphasize the main outcomes and lessons learned. Tailoring the report to different audiences—such as staff, funders, and community members—ensures that your information is understandable and relevant to all stakeholders.

Using Findings for Improvement

The main goal of the evaluation is to utilize the findings to enhance the project and guide future initiatives. You should share the outcomes with stakeholders, discuss their implications, and develop action plans to address any identified issues. Establishing continuous feedback loops will enable you to refine and polish your strategies, ensuring sustained effectiveness and impact.

Identifying Relevant Performance Indicators and Metrics

Identifying relevant performance indicators and metrics is another component of evaluating your projects. These indicators will be your benchmarks to measure progress, results, and overall impact, allowing you to evaluate effectiveness, make informed decisions, and refine techniques. You can identify and select these performance indicators and metrics by doing the following.

Understand the Project's Goals and Objectives

Identifying relevant performance indicators begins with thoroughly understanding your project's objectives and goals.

Engage Stakeholders

You need to engage stakeholders, including staff, volunteers, funders, and beneficiaries in the selection phase. Stakeholders can give you valuable insights into what success looks like from different eyes. This collaboration also ensures that the selected indicators are not only relevant but also comprehensive. Surveys, interviews, and focus groups can be used to effectively collect stakeholder input.

Categorize Indicators

Performance indicators can be classified into three primary types:

- **Input indicators:** These measure the resources utilized to implement a project, such as staff time, materials, and funding. For instance, the number of volunteer hours contributed to a community clean-up initiative.

- **Output indicators:** These measure the direct services or products the project delivers; for example, the number of meals served in a food program.

- **Outcome indicators:** These measure both the short- and long-term outcomes of the project. They evaluate changes in behavior, knowledge, or conditions resulting from the project, like improved literacy rates among participants in an education-associated program.

Select Specific, Relevant Indicators

Every project objective needs to have specific performance indicators directly linked to it. These indicators should be relevant and aligned with the intended results. For example

- **Education programs:** Indicators may include graduation rates, attendance rates, test scores, and literacy levels.

- **Health programs:** Indicators may include the number of health screenings conducted, alterations in health behaviors, incidence rates of targeted illnesses, and participant health results.

- **Environmental programs:** Indicators may include the amount of waste recycled, water- or air-quality enhancements, and biodiversity levels.

Ensure Measurability and Feasibility

Indicators must be measurable using available methods and tools. It is vital to consider the feasibility of data collection, making sure that the necessary time, expertise, and resources are available. For instance, measuring participant satisfaction through surveys will be feasible if you can administer and analyze these surveys consistently.

Align With Industry Standards and Best Practices

Aligning performance indicators with industry standards as well as best practices can enhance comparability and credibility. Many sectors have set frameworks and recommended indicators. For example, the Global Reporting Initiative gives standardized metrics for sustainability reporting, and the Centers for Disease Control and Prevention (CDC) provides guidelines for health program evaluations (Hussey et al., 2001).

Use a Balanced Approach

A balanced set of indicators gives a holistic view of project performance. This is about having a mix of qualitative and quantitative indicators, encompassing narrative insights and numerical data. Quantitative indicators, like the number of beneficiaries served, give objective measurements, while qualitative indicators, like beneficiary testimonials, offer depth and context to the quantitative data.

Regularly Review and Update Indicators

Performance indicators must be regularly revised and updated to mirror changes in project objectives, external conditions, and stakeholder needs. Continuous improvement procedures, such as after-action evaluations or annual reviews, help guarantee that the indicators remain effective and relevant.

Establish Baselines and Targets

Setting baselines and targets for each indicator helps when you want to measure progress. A baseline offers a point of reference from which the change would be measured, while targets set measurable and specific goals for what the project aims to attain. For instance, if the baseline literacy rate in a community is 50%, a target can be to enhance it to 75% within 2 years.

Document and Communicate the Indicators

Documenting and effectively communicating the chosen performance indicators and metrics to all stakeholders ensures that you adhere to transparency and shared understanding. Clear documentation must include definitions, data collection methods, data sources, and reporting timelines. Regular communication, like through progress reports and stakeholder meetings, keeps everyone engaged and informed.

Communicating the Potential Impact and Significance of the Proposed Project

Effectively communicating your expected impact and the importance of a proposed project helps you secure funding, garner support, and ensure stakeholder engagement. This refers not only to detailing the potential outcomes and benefits but also to conveying the bigger picture and the significance of your project within the field or community.

To grasp the importance of communicating the expected impact and significance of a proposed project, let us follow the journey of a nonprofit, Charity: Water. It is a nonprofit organization committed to offering clean drinking water to people in developing countries.

Understanding the Issue

The mission of Charity: Water is to address a critical global issue: the lack of access to safe and clean drinking water. It communicates the importance of this problem by underlining stark statistics—663 million people worldwide lack access to clean water, which then results in a host of health conditions, educational barriers, and economic challenges (Hutton & Chase, 2017). By framing the issue with such persuasive data, Charity: Water highlights the importance and urgency of its work, making it crystal clear why its proposed projects are important.

Articulating the Vision and Goals

It is critical to present a clear and inspiring vision by communicating the potential impact. Charity: Water pictures a world where everyone can easily access clean water. Its specific objective consists of providing sustainable water solutions to needy communities and guaranteeing that each dollar donated goes directly to funding these initiatives. This clear articulation of vision and objectives helps stakeholders view the organization's aims and its strategies to achieve them.

Using Data and Evidence

Quantitative and qualitative data and evidence are useful tools for explaining the potential output of a project. Charity: Water leverages a wealth of data to illustrate the influence of its interventions. It cites metrics such as the population served, the number of wells constructed, and improvements in health and productivity in communities where it has completed projects. For instance, it might present data demonstrating that in a village where a new well was installed, waterborne illnesses were reduced by 40%, school attendance among girls increased by 40%, and local businesses saw a 30% rise in productivity due to the availability of clean water.

Sharing Stories of Change

Personal stories and testimonials can help you make the impact relatable and tangible. Charity: Water frequently includes stories of individuals and communities who benefitted from its projects. These stories helped it humanize the data, making the project's potential impact clearer and emotionally compelling.

Highlighting the Broader Impact

It is also crucial to communicate the ripple effects of your project. Charity: Water focuses on how clean water has impacted several aspects of community life, including but not limited to education, health, and economic development. It further explains how access to clean water minimizes the disease burden, which, in turn, decreases healthcare costs as well as absenteeism from school and work. Enhanced water access can free up time for children and women and allow them to pursue education and more economic opportunities. By painting a vivid picture of these broader benefits, Charity: Water demonstrates how its projects can contribute to sustainable and long-term development.

Building Trust and Credibility

Transparency and accountability are the backbone of cultivating trust with stakeholders. Charity: Water uses innovative ways to show exactly how donations are utilized. It gives GPS coordinates and photos of completed projects, ensuring that donors can see the direct influence of their contributions. This level of transparency creates credibility and reassures its stakeholders that their support is making a tangible difference.

Engaging and Mobilizing Supporters

Ultimately, effective communication must inspire action. Charity: Water accomplishes this by engaging its supporters through compelling calls to action, whether it is fundraising, donating, or spreading the word. This fosters a sense of community and shared purpose, encouraging individuals to join this movement and contribute to a lasting cause.

Chapter 6:

Writing Style and Presentation

In the dynamic world of innovation and technology, securing funding through well-crafted grant proposals has become essential for driving progress and achieving meaningful results. Picture a world where groundbreaking research, transformative community initiatives, and pioneering educational initiatives blossom, unhampered by financial restrictions. This is the promise that a well-crafted grant proposal holds—a bridge between imagined ideas and tangible, real-world change.

Effective formatting and structuring of a grant proposal are crucial for ensuring maximum impact and readability. A well-organized proposal not only makes it easier for reviewers to understand your project but also demonstrates your professionalism and attention to detail. Here are key components and strategies for structuring your grant proposal, along with examples for clarity.

Just like turning a blank canvas into a masterpiece, the journey of a grant proposal starts with a captivating introduction, setting the stage for the entire narrative. Here, much like in a piece of artwork, you distill the essence of your project into a story that captivates, informs, and persuades. Your proposal should aim to address a critical issue that reverberates within your community and beyond. At its heart lies a commitment to fostering innovation, nurturing sustainability, and improving the quality of life for countless people.

In this chapter, we will discuss the specifics of writing style and presentation for your grant proposals.

Writing Clear, Concise, and Persuasive Grant Proposals

Writing a clear, concise, and persuasive grant proposal will help you secure funding and ensure the success of your projects across a wide range of fields. A well-crafted proposal communicates the significance and feasibility of a project as well as inspires enthusiasm and confidence in potential funders.

You can employ these key strategies to help you write effective grant proposals.

Clarity in Objectives and Goals

A grant proposal begins with a clear statement of goals and objectives. Funders need to comprehend exactly what you want to achieve and why it matters.

Example: "Our project aims to decrease childhood obesity in the local community by 15% over the next year through a detailed health and nutrition education program in schools."

This objective is SMART and offers a clear project target.

Conciseness in Language

Brevity is vital in grant proposals. Avoid slang and unnecessary details that can confuse or bore the reader. Rather than that, focus on presenting important information succinctly.

Example: "To address childhood obesity, our initiative will implement a series of interactive workshops, give healthy meal plans, and establish after-school physical activity clubs."

This sentence is clear and straightforward and conveys the main program activities without an influx of information.

Persuasive Storytelling

Incorporating storytelling elements can also make your proposal more persuasive and engaging. Share a compelling narrative that demonstrates the problem and the outcome your project will have.

Example: "Last year, Alina, a 10-year-old student, struggled with her weight and faced bullying at school. Through our program, she learned about healthy eating and started participating in many physical activities. Today, Alina is healthier, more confident, and thriving academically. We want to replicate Alina's success story for thousands of other children in our community."

This story has personalized the issue and explains the project's positive effects, making the proposal more impactful.

Detailed Budget and Justification

Funders also want to see a well-structured budget that justifies each expense. Break down the costs succinctly and explain why each item is required for the project's success.

Example: "Our budget includes $15,000 for educational materials, $6,000 for workshop facilitators, and $2,000 for sports equipment. Educational materials are essential for giving accurate health information, workshop facilitators are required for effective program delivery, and sports equipment will encourage physical activities that promote fitness and well-being."

This breakdown illustrates that you have thoughtfully considered each part of the project and ensured transparency in how funds will be utilized.

Evidence of Need and Impact

Moreover, provide data and evidence to support why your project is needed and its anticipated impact. Use research findings, statistics, and testimonials to strengthen your case.

Example: "According to the County Health Rankings, we have a childhood obesity rate of 20%, much higher than the national average of 18%. Research by the CDC shows that comprehensive school-based programs can lower obesity rates by up to 15%. Stories from our pilot program participants disclose improvements in not only physical health but also academic performance."

This example merges research, statistics, and testimonials to build a robust argument for the project's necessity and potential effectiveness.

Strong Organizational Capability

Show that your organization has the skill and capacity to successfully execute the project. Highlight relevant experience, past successes, and qualifications of main team members.

Example: "Our organization has over 15 years of experience in community health projects, successfully implementing similar projects in four neighboring cities. Our team consists of Dr. Jane Smith, a renowned public health professional, and John Doe, an expert project manager, both of whom have directed many successful health campaigns."

By showcasing the track record of your organization and the qualifications of your team, you can build credibility and reassure your funders that their investment will be well-managed.

Clear Evaluation Plan

Summarize how you will measure the success of your program. Define the metrics as well as methods you will employ to evaluate outcomes and ensure accountability.

Example: "We will measure our program's success by tracking changes in BMI among our participants, surveying parents and students about their health habits, and analyzing the records of school attendance. Regular reports will also be submitted to our funders, documenting progress and any required adjustments."

A clear evaluation plan will demonstrate your commitment to transparency and continuous learning and improvements, further building funder confidence.

Formatting and Structuring the Proposal for Maximum Impact

Effective formatting and structuring of a grant proposal ensures maximum impact as well as readability. A well-organized proposal makes it easier for reviewers to comprehend your project and demonstrates your professionalism and attention to detail.

Here are the main components and strategies for structuring your grant proposal.

Title Page

Your title page should be professional and clean, offering essential information at a glance.

Example

Title: Sustainable Futures Initiative

Submitted by: Future Health Organization

Contact Person: Dr. Jane Smith

Address: 123 ABC Lane, Eco City, State, ZIP

Email: jsmith@greenearth.xyz

Phone: (123) 456-7890

Date: June 22, 2024

This page contains the project title, organization name, contact information, and submission date, presenting a polished first impression.

Executive Summary

The executive summary provides a concise overview of your proposal, stressing the key points.

Example

"The Sustainable Futures Initiative strives to lower the impact of climate change on our local farming community through renewable energy solutions, community education, and sustainable agricultural practices. Over 3 years, we aim to train 300 farmers, install solar panels on 60 farms, and reach 2,000 residents through workshops. This $500,000 project will enhance sustainability and resilience in Eco City."

The summary is concise and offers an overview of goals, methods, expected outcomes, and budget, enticing the reader to explore further.

Problem Statement

Distinctly define the problem your project addresses, supported by both data and evidence.

Example

"Eco City faces growing challenges from climate change, such as frequent floods and droughts. The local farming community, representing 40% of the population, has seen almost a 30% decline in crop yields over the past 4 years. According to the County Environmental Report (2023), these adverse conditions threaten not only food security but also economic stability. Immediate action is required to reduce these effects and encourage long-term sustainability."

This section clearly states the problem, backed by reports and statistics, emphasizing the importance and urgency of the project.

Goals and Objectives

Define what you aim to accomplish with your project using SMART goals.

Example

- **Goal:** "Increase the resilience of Eco City's farming community to climate change."

- **Objectives:**
    - "Train 300 farmers in sustainable agricultural practices within 3 years."
    - "Install solar panels on 60 farms to decrease dependence on nonrenewable energy sources."

- "Conduct 20 community workshops reaching 2,000 residents to facilitate climate awareness and sustainable living."

This section outlines specific objectives that guide the project and allow for the measurement of success.

Project Description

Describe the activities and methods you will employ to achieve your objectives.

Example

1. **Sustainable agricultural training:** "Partnering with local agricultural experts, we will conduct bimonthly training sessions covering water management, crop diversification, and soil conservation."

2. **Renewable energy installation:** "Collaborate with SolarTech Solutions to equip 60 farms with solar panels, minimizing energy costs, and carbon footprint."

3. **Community workshops:** "Organize bimonthly workshops in collaboration with Eco City Schools, emphasizing climate change impacts and sustainable practices, with interactive sessions for hands-on learning."

This section will provide a clear roadmap of all activities, illustrating thorough feasibility and planning.

Budget

Present a detailed budget that justifies each expense.

Example

Item	Cost ($)
Sustainable agriculture training	100,000
Solar panel installation	250,000
Community workshops	40,000
Project management	60,000
Evaluation and reporting	25,000
Contingency	25,000
Total	**500,000**

This detailed budget table guarantees transparency and also shows funders exactly how their money will be utilized.

Evaluation Plan

Describe how you will measure the success of your project.

Example

"We will measure our progress through quarterly surveys and reports to track:

- number of farmers trained
- farmer's usage of new practices
- energy savings and decreased carbon emissions from solar panel installations
- participant feedback and knowledge gained from workshops

Besides this, an independent evaluator will conduct an annual assessment to recommend improvements and overall impact."

This section recapitulates specific metrics and methods for evaluating your project's effectiveness. It also ensures accountability.

Organizational Capability

Shed light on not only your organization's qualifications but also your experience relevant to the project.

Example

"Green Earth Organization has over a decade of experience in environmental sustainability projects. Our past projects, such as the Green Schools Program, successfully minimized energy use in local schools by 35%. Our team includes Dr. Jane Smith, an environmental scientist with 20 years of experience, and John Doe, a seasoned project manager. Together, they have guided multiple projects to successful completion."

You build credibility and trust with funders by showcasing your expertise and previous successes.

Conclusion

Summarize your proposal, reiterating its significance and inviting support.

Example

"The Sustainable Futures Initiative symbolizes a crucial step toward securing Eco City's future against the harmful impacts of climate change. By investing in sustainable practices as well as community education, we can create a model of sustainability and resilience. We invite you to support our transformative project, joining us in our devotion to a healthier and more sustainable future."

This final section should reinforce your proposal's importance and make a compelling case for support.

Formatting Tips

- **Use headings and subheadings:** Clearly labeled sections will make your document easy to navigate.

- **Bullet points and numbered lists:** These will help you break down information into digestible chunks.

- **Consistent font and style:** Ensure that you use a professional font (e.g., Calibri, Times New Roman, or Arial) and consistent formatting throughout.

- **Visual aids:** Charts, images, and graphs can describe points and add visual interest.

By adhering to these formatting and structuring guidelines, you can craft a grant proposal that is clear, persuasive, and concise; thereby maximizing its impact and increasing the likelihood of securing funding.

Editing and Proofreading for Accuracy and Professionalism

Editing and proofreading are important steps when you are creating the grant proposal during the writing phase. Ensuring your proposal is professional, free from errors, and accurate can largely enhance its effectiveness and credibility. Here's a comprehensive guide on how to edit and proofread your grant proposal, complete with examples for clarity.

Review for Clarity and Consistency

Make sure that objectives are clearly stated and that your message is conveyed consistently. For example, if your objective stated in the introduction part is to reduce obesity by 25%, ensure this target is consistently referenced throughout your proposal.

Check for Grammar and Spelling Errors

Always ensure that your proposal is free from grammatical errors. Avoid spelling mistakes. You can use tools, such as Grammarly or built-in spell checkers in word processors; however, also do a manual proofread at the end.

Verify Data and Facts

Most importantly, make sure that your data is accurate and that you have properly cited. For example, if you write, "According to the County Health Rankings, we have a childhood obesity rate of 23%," ensure that you double-check the source to confirm the accuracy of this fact.

Maintain a Professional Tone and Language

While writing a grant proposal, use a professional tone and formal language. For instance, rather than using "kids," write "children" and use "numerous benefits" instead of "lots of benefits."

Consistency in Formatting

Make sure that your proposal has uniform formatting. Also, check for consistent font sizes and types, spacing, and heading styles.

For instance, if you are using bullet points for listing goals, you should use the same bullet style and indentation throughout the whole document.

Logical Flow and Structure

Moreover, follow a logical flow. Make sure that your problem statement logically contributes to the proposed solution, and that your methodology flows naturally from the goals.

Proofreading Techniques

Read aloud your proposal. When you read your proposal out loud, it helps you catch awkward errors and phrasing that you can overlook otherwise. For example, reading, "The initiative will involve numerous community members to participate in," can reveal that it should be, "The initiative will involve numerous community members participating."

Use the Track Changes Feature

You need to enable track changes in your word processor to not only keep a record of edits but also confirm that nothing significant is accidentally removed.

When you are editing a sentence for clarity, you should see the deleted and added words or sentences.

Peer Review

Have your colleagues review your proposal to offer fresh perspectives and catch errors you might have overlooked or missed.

Let us further comprehend this topic with the help of an example:

- **Original text:** "Our project wants to increase child health by giving educational programs. We will focus on physical activity and nutrition. By making kids learn healthy habits, we are hoping to reduce the rates of obesity in the local area."

- **Edited version:** "Our project aims to improve children's health by providing comprehensive educational programs focused on physical activity and nutrition. By teaching children healthy habits, we hope to lower obesity rates in the local community."

Editing Steps

1. **Clarity and consistency:** Changed "increase child health" to "improve children's health" for more clarity and consistency.

2. **Professional language:** Replaced "kids" with "children" to establish a professional tone.

3. **Logical flow:** Combined the first two sentences for a seamless logical flow: "We will focus on physical activity and nutrition. By teaching children healthy habits..."

Checklist for Final Review

Lastly, use the following checklist when you are finished proofreading your document.

- **Content review:**
    - Are your objectives and goals clear and consistent?
    - Is this problem statement well-supported by data?
    - Are the proposed methods and activities logically structured?

- **Language and style:**
    - Is the language professional and formal?
    - Are there any spelling or grammar errors?
    - Is there any jargon that needs removal or simplification?

- **Formatting and presentation:**
    - Are headings and subheadings used correctly?
    - Is the formatting consistent, such as spacing, fonts, and bullet points?
    - Are visual aids relevant and clear?

- **Accuracy and proofreading:**
    - Are all data and facts accurate and cited correctly?
    - Have you read the document aloud?
    - Have you asked a friend or colleague to review it?
    - Have all track changes and comments been addressed and resolved?

By editing and proofreading your grant proposal, you ensure that it is professional, polished, and persuasive, greatly multiplying its chances of success.

Chapter 7:

Submission and Follow-up

When you submit a grant proposal, it signals the beginning of a dynamic, transformative journey ahead. Imagine the excitement and anticipation as your crafted proposal lands in the hands of those who hold the key to funding your innovative project. This very moment is not only pivotal but also encapsulates months of meticulous planning, collaborative efforts, and solid research. However, securing a grant is not only about a strong proposal—it requires strategic follow-up so that you may ensure your project stands out in a competitive landscape.

When you prepare for submission, it becomes imperative to adopt a proactive approach. Beyond hitting the send button, you should consider the significance of a well-timed follow-up that reinforces your project's urgency and relevance. A thoughtful follow-up showcases your commitment and professionalism as well as keeps your proposal top-of-mind for your reviewers. Moreover, it is an opportunity to cultivate relationships, address any potential concerns or queries, and reaffirm your project's alignment with your funder's objectives.

In this chapter, we will explore the effective practices for submitting your grant proposal and formulating effective follow-up strategies. From making sure that all submission guidelines are meticulously followed to customizing your follow-up communications, these crucial steps will help you navigate the post-submission period with confidence and multiply your chances of success.

Reviewing Submission Guidelines and Requirements

Adhering to submission guidelines is a way to confirm that your proposal is considered by the funding agency and illustrates your attention to detail as well as respect for their processes.

Carefully Read the Request for Proposal or Request for Application

Request-for-proposal (RFP) or request-for-application (RFA) documents have specific guidelines for submitting a particular proposal. These documents discuss what the funder expects and how they want to acquire your proposal (Universal Services Administrative Co., n.d.).

For example, a typical RFP can include sections on funding priorities, deadlines, application components, eligibility criteria, and submission instructions. Reading the whole document thoroughly can help you understand your funder's priorities and whether your project aligns with their objectives.

Eligibility Criteria

Before investing your time in creating a proposal, ensure your project and organization meet the eligibility criteria. These criteria can contain factors such as geographic location, type of organization (for-profit, educational institution, or nonprofit,), and clear project focus areas. For example, if an RFP outlines that only educational institutions within a certain state qualify, a nonprofit organization in a different state would not be eligible. Ensuring eligibility will save you time and effort.

Funding Priorities and Objectives

Understanding your funder's objectives and priorities allows you to customize your proposal to meet their interests. Underlining how your project aligns with those priorities enhances your chances of success. For example, If your foundation's priority is to support innovative educational technology, your proposal must clearly illustrate how your project uses cutting-edge technology to maximize educational outcomes.

Application Components

Submission guidelines sometimes list the required components of the application, ranging from an executive summary, project narrative, and a cover letter to letters of support, budget, and organizational documents. A federal grant, for example, can require a detailed project narrative, a sustainability plan, a logic model, and an assessment plan; however, a private foundation can have a simpler requirement of budget and a cover letter.

Formatting Requirements

Many funders specify formatting requirements, like font size and type, page limits, margin width, and how to structure headings as well as subheadings. Adhering to these requirements is critical. Take the example of an RFP as it might state that your proposal should be written in 12-point Times New Roman font, with 1-in. margins, and must not exceed 10 pages. Submissions that do not adhere to these guidelines might be disqualified.

Submission Process

Additionally, determine whether your proposal must be submitted in hard copy or electronically. For electronic submissions, you will need to familiarize yourself with the submission portal along with any technical requirements.

Some funders also use specific online systems, such as Grants.gov for federal grants, while others may demand email submissions. Ensure you comprehend the process and test the submission system if possible to avoid errors or last-minute issues.

Deadlines

Always pay attention to the submission deadlines and any deadlines for queries or clarifications. Missing a deadline can result in automatic disqualification. Therefore, it is wise if you plan to submit at least two days before to buffer against any unexpected issues.

Additional Review and Checklist

You can create a checklist based on the submission guidelines. It will help you ensure that all components are included and formatted correctly.

To get an idea, your checklist should include items such as Executive Summary (1 page), Project Narrative (11 pages), Letters of Support (3), and Budget (Excel format)."

Final Review

Lastly, you must conduct a final review. Before the submission, go through the entire proposal and checklist to make sure everything is complete and follows the guidelines. Again, consider having a colleague review your proposal to catch any missed details.

Correcting issues (if any) before submission will ensure that your proposal is compliant.

By meticulously reviewing submission guidelines as well as requirements, you illustrate professionalism and increase the chances that your proposal will be considered favorably. This thoroughness also mirrors your organization's capability and preparedness to execute the proposed project successfully.

Assembling and Submitting the Grant Proposal Package

Assembling and submitting a grant proposal package is a vital step that demands your attention to detail and adherence to the funder's specific instructions or guidelines. You can effectively assemble and submit your grant proposal package by following the steps below.

Gather Required Documents

Identify and gather all important components. Then, compile all the necessary documents specified in the submission guidelines. This usually includes several main elements:

- **Cover letter:** Introduce your project and organization, then formally request for funding.

- **Executive summary:** Give a concise overview of your project.

- **Project narrative:** Provide a detailed explanation of the goals, problem, methodology, and expected results.

- **Budget and budget justification:** Show a detailed financial plan for your project and explain how funds will be utilized.

- **Organizational information:** Provide background, mission, and relevant experience of your organization.

- **Letters of support:** Endorsements from stakeholders or partners that underline support for the project should be supplied.

- **Appendices:** Add any additional materials, such as project timelines, resumes of key staff, or detailed evaluation plans.

Format and Organize the Documents

Always follow formatting guidelines. Ensure that all your documents follow the specific formatting requirements described in the submission guidelines.

You can use consistent headers and footers along with page numbers for easier navigation.

Also, arrange all the documents in the order specified by your funder. This typically reflects the order listed in the submission process. For example:

1. Cover letter
2. Executive summary
3. Project narrative
4. Budget and budget justification
5. Organizational information
6. Letters of support
7. Appendices

Review for Completeness and Accuracy

Double-check that you have all the documents and that each one is accurate and complete. In addition to this, make sure that all information is consistent across all documents.

For instance, you should verify that the budget figures in the budget justification match those explained in the project summary and narrative. Most importantly, double-check to see that all letters of support are not only correctly addressed but also signed.

Prepare for Submission

Determine the right method for submission, and follow the instructions precisely.

For Electronic Submission

- **Create PDF files:** Convert all your documents to PDF to ensure consistent formatting.

- **Label files clearly:** Use descriptive and clear filenames like "Organization_Name_Project_Narrative.pdf"

- **Upload to the portal:** Log in to the submission portal, upload files, and confirm the successful upload.

For Hard Copy Submission

- **Print and assemble:** Print all your documents in high-quality printouts. Assemble them in the specified order.

- **Bind or clip:** Utilize a binder clip or other methods as instructed to keep documents organized.

- **Mail:** Send it via a reliable courier service, and ensure it is scheduled to arrive before the deadline.

Confirm Submission

After you have submitted, confirm receipt of your proposal. You can look for an automatic confirmation email from the submission portal. If you have not received any confirmation, follow up with the funder to verify that your proposal was received.

In the case of hard copies, you can use a courier service that offers delivery confirmation.

Follow Up

Prepare to follow up with your funder after submission to express continued interest and address any questions they might have. Consider waiting a week after the submission deadline and then send a polite email to the funder's contact person, confirming receipt and your willingness to provide any additional information or clarification where needed.

Maintain Records

Always have copies of all submitted documents for your records. You can store digital copies in a dedicated folder on your computer and backup system. Keep hard copies in a labeled file folder for easy and immediate reference.

Following Up With Funders and Maintaining Communication

After submitting your grant proposal, consider sending a follow-up email or making a phone call to confirm receipt. A concise and polite message is ideal, reaffirming your interest in the funding opportunity.

Moreover, during the review process, you should maintain regular but not intrusive communication. Sometimes, funders offer timelines for the review process; respect these timelines and avoid excessive queries. A well-timed follow-up, like a short email halfway through the expected review period, can be best to reaffirm your interest and give any new and relevant updates about your project or organization.

If your funder has requested additional clarification or information, respond promptly and thoroughly. Timely responses show your organization's reliability and readiness. Ensure that all additional information given is accurate and aligns with the main proposal.

Despite the outcome, always show gratitude for the opportunity to apply. If your proposal is successful, you can send a thank-you note and confirm the next steps, such as any requirements for fund reporting and disbursement. However, if the proposal is not funded, a gracious thank-you note will leave a positive impression and can open doors for future proposals. Also, inquire about feedback to identify areas for improvement in future proposals.

You can use the review process as an opportunity to cultivate a long-term relationship with the funder. Prioritize to attend any offered networking webinars, meetings, and events. Expressing ongoing interest and engagement in the funder's activities and mission can foster a positive relationship, doubling your chances for funding opportunities and future collaborations.

Chapter 8:

Overcoming Common Challenges and Pitfalls

Grant writing also presents many challenges and obstacles that can impede the success of securing funding. Addressing these common issues effectively can enhance the quality of your proposals and your chances of success.

So, without further delay, let us learn how to overcome these challenges.

Addressing Common Challenges and Obstacles in Grant Writing

Understanding Funder Requirements

One of the main challenges is thoroughly understanding and meeting your funder's requirements. This involves comprehending the guidelines and ensuring your project aligns with their priorities. Misinterpretation of requirements can contribute to disqualification. To overcome this, always carefully read the RFP multiple times, develop a checklist of requirements, and design your proposal to match the funder's goals precisely.

Developing a Clear and Compelling Narrative

Creating a clear and compelling narrative is another main obstacle. A well-written proposal should narrate a cohesive story that highlights the problem, proposed solution, and expected outcomes. Some proposals fail because they fail to engage their target reader. To address this, use a structured format, maintain consistency in messaging, and use persuasive language to convey the importance of your project.

Demonstrating Impact and Sustainability

Funders want to understand the potential impact along with the sustainability of your project. Talking about measurable outcomes and long-term benefits can be difficult. To deal with this, include specific, quantifiable objectives, and offer a detailed evaluation plan. Outline any past successes and a realistic sustainability plan that tells how the project will continue after the end of the grant period.

Competition and Limited Funding

Another constant challenge is a high level of competition for limited funding. Many worthy projects are competing for the same funds, making it vital to stand out. To tackle this, make sure that your proposal is well-researched, customized to the specific funder, and error-free. Building relationships with funders and comprehending their specific interests can also give your proposal an edge.

Time Management

Undoubtedly, grant writing is a time-intensive procedure. Balancing grant writing with other obligations can be demanding. Effective time management and planning are crucial. Begin the process early, develop internal deadlines, and break the proposal into small, manageable sections. Employing a team approach, where different team members deal with different sections, can also help divide the workload.

Strategies for Navigating Rejection and Learning From Feedback

When you are seeking a grant, know that you can also face some rejection. Rejection does not mean you should stop; rather, it is synonymous with a learning opportunity.

Below are the main strategies for dealing with rejection and using feedback effectively:

- **Accept rejection gracefully:** Rejection is a common factor in the grant-writing process. Accept it with professionalism. Do not take it personally and know that many factors can impact funding decisions, sometimes unrelated to the quality of your proposal.

- **Request feedback:** Politely ask your funder for detailed feedback on your proposal. Understanding the reasons behind the rejection can give important insights for future applications. Funders can offer constructive criticism regarding areas like clarity, feasibility, budget details, or alignment with priorities.

- **Analyze feedback:** Thoroughly review feedback. Identify specific areas of weakness or common themes mentioned by many reviewers. This analysis will help you decide where improvements are needed.

- **Revise and improve:** Use the feedback to strengthen your proposal. Focus on addressing the specific problems stressed by reviewers.

- **Enhance your skills:** Consider professional development or additional training in areas where feedback suggests a need for improvement. Workshops, courses, or webinars in grant writing, budgeting, or program assessment can hone your skills and boost your competitiveness.

- **Seek alternative funding sources:** You can use your rejected proposal for other funding opportunities. Research other funders whose priorities can better align with your project. Customize your revised proposal to fit their specific objectives and guidelines.

- **Maintain relationships:** Stay connected with your funders who rejected your proposal. Extend your gratitude for their consideration as well as feedback.

- **Reflect and adapt:** Reflect on the whole process starting from preparation to submission. Identify what worked well and what did not. Adapt your strategies based on this reflection and the received feedback. Continuous improvement is essential for long-term success in grant writing.

Tips for Staying Motivated and Resilient

Although staying motivated and resilient in the process of grant writing can be challenging, it is important for long-term success. Use these practical tips to maintain your drive and resilience:

- **Set clear goals:** break down the entire grant-writing process into smaller and more manageable tasks. Setting clear and achievable objectives for each stage can make the process less overwhelming and help you track your progress.

- **Celebrate small wins:** Celebrate small milestones, like completing a draft or submitting a proposal. These small wins can not only boost your morale but also keep you motivated.

- **Maintain a positive mindset:** Focus on the impact of your project instead of on the possibility of rejection. Remember, every proposal offers you an opportunity to refine your ideas and enhance your grant-writing skills.

- **Seek support and collaboration:** Engage with your colleagues or join grant-writing groups. Sharing challenges, experiences, and successes with others can offer emotional support and advice, making the process feel less solitary.

- **Learn continuously:** View every experience, whether a rejection or a success, as a learning opportunity. Use feedback to polish your skills and approach, turning failures into growth opportunities.

- **Take care of yourself:** Ensure you are managing stress by practicing self-care, taking regular breaks, and maintaining a healthy work-life balance. Regular exercise, relaxation, and adequate rest are important for sustaining long-term motivation as well as resilience.

Chapter 9:

Case Studies and Examples

As we are about to end this journey, it is time that we look at some real-world examples of organizations that successfully secured funding.

By exploring real-world examples of successful grant proposals, you will learn many valuable insights into what can help you make your proposal stand out. By examining the main elements that lead to their success, such as innovative approaches, robust evaluation plans, and clear objectives, we can identify best practices as well as strategies to apply to your own grant-writing endeavors.

So, let us look at some case studies to learn from them.

Real-World Examples of Successful Grant Proposals

Community Health Initiative

- **Project:** Healthy Kids, Healthy Communities
- **Organization:** Local Health Coalition
- **Funder:** Robert Wood Johnson Foundation
- **Objective:** To decrease childhood obesity in underserved communities by executing community-based health programs (Strunk & Bussel, 2015).

Key Elements for Success

1. **Clear problem statement:** The proposal talked about the rising rates of childhood obesity in the targeted communities, further backed up by local health statistics and national data.

2. **Strong objectives:** The objectives were measurable and specific, aiming to lower obesity rates by 10% over 3 years through physical activity programs, community gardens, and nutrition education (Strunk & Bussel, 2015).

3. **Collaborative approach:** The proposal also outlined partnerships with local schools, health clinics, and community centers. These collaborations showed a community-wide commitment as well as shared resources.

4. **Sustainability plan:** The plan consisted of training community members to continue the programs post-funding, supporting long-term impact.

5. **Detailed budget:** A detailed and transparent budget highlighted expenses for staffing, program activities, evaluation, and materials (Strunk & Bussel, 2015).

Outcome

The proposal successfully received full funding, contributing to the successful implementation of many health programs. Over the last three years, the initiative reported a substantial reduction in childhood obesity rates, aligning with the project's goals (Strunk & Bussel, 2015).

Environmental Conservation Effort

- **Project:** Save Our Wetlands
- **Organization:** Green Earth Alliance
- **Funder:** Environmental Protection Agency (EPA)

- **Objective:** To protect and restore wetland ecosystems in a targeted conservation area (EPA, 2023).

Key Elements for Success

1. **Urgent need and impact:** The proposal effectively communicated the immediate need for wetland conservation, further explained by environmental impact studies and data on declining biodiversity.

2. **Clear goals and methods:** Specific goals included eliminating invasive species, monitoring wildlife populations, and replanting native vegetation. Detailed methodologies for each activity were offered.

3. **Expert team:** The project team included conservationists, volunteers, and ecologists, with relevant experience; thereby, adding credibility to the proposal (EPA, 2023).

4. **Public engagement:** The proposal entailed educational programs for both local schools and community members to spread awareness about wetland conservation.

5. **Long-term vision:** A vision for the long-term ecological health of the wetlands, including ongoing maintenance and monitoring, was vividly stated.

Outcome

The EPA grant allowed for important restoration activities, enhancing wetland health and enriching biodiversity. The project also improved community awareness and participation in environmental conservation (EPA, 2023).

Analysis of Effective Strategies and Techniques

Successful grant proposals often share effective strategies and techniques that can largely enhance their appeal to funders. Let us analyze these main elements:

- **Clear and compelling problem statement:**
    - **Effective strategy:** A clear and compelling problem statement is essential. It explains the issue your project aims to address, supported by relevant evidence and data. This also helps funders understand the significance and urgency of the situation.
    - **Technique:** Use case studies, expert testimonials, and statistics to explain the problem's impact.

- **Alignment with funder priorities:**
    - **Effective strategy:** Tailoring your proposal to align with the funder's priorities and mission multiplies the chances of success. Funders are more likely to support initiatives and projects that align with their values and goals.
    - **Technique:** Highlight how your specific project aligns with these priorities in the narrative and the executive summary.

- **Specific and measurable objectives:**
    - **Effective strategy:** Well-defined objectives need to be SMART, as they make your proposal more focused and credible.
    - **Technique:** Break down your objectives into small, clear, and actionable steps. Use correct and precise language to define success and how it will be evaluated.

- **Detailed and realistic budget:**
    - o **Effective strategy:** A clear and detailed budget illustrates that you have carefully crafted your project and understand the financial requirements.
    - o **Technique:** Include a budget narrative that describes each line item. Ensure that your costs are justified and realistic, reflecting the true needs of the project.

- **Strong evaluation plan:**
    - o **Effective strategy:** An effective evaluation plan shows how you will evaluate your project's success. It assures funders that outcomes will be assessed and that there will be accountability.
    - o **Technique:** Detail all the methods you will employ to evaluate progress and outcomes. You can include timelines and responsible personnel for each evaluation activity as well.

- **Sustainability plan:**
    - o **Effective strategy:** A sustainability plan will show how your project will continue after the end of the grant period. This also reassures your funders that their investment will have a lasting impact.
    - o **Technique:** Recognize potential future funding sources, revenue-generating activities, and partnerships. Discuss plans for scaling the project and cultivating capacity within your organization.

Lessons Learned and Insights From Grant-Writing Experiences

- **Start early and plan ahead:** Start your grant-writing process early, as it gives you ample time to create a comprehensive proposal, assemble necessary documents, and seek feedback. Rushed proposals are usually less compelling and incomplete.

- **Engage stakeholders and partners:** Collaborating with partners and stakeholders can strengthen your proposal. Their input merged with support can double your project's feasibility and credibility. Engage them early to incorporate their perspectives and secure letters of support.

- **Seek feedback and revise:** Drafting a proposal is only the beginning. Seek feedback from mentors, grant-writing professionals, or colleagues. Next, revise your proposal based on this feedback to bring further clarity and effectiveness.

- **Stay persistent and resilient:** Grant writing sometimes involves facing rejections. Each rejection should be seen as an opportunity to learn and grow. Analyzing feedback from unsuccessful applications can help you gain valuable insights for future proposals. Staying resilient and persistent is key to long-term success.

- **Develop strong relationships with funders:** Cultivating and maintaining relationships with funders can largely enhance your chances of success. Engage with their initiatives, attend their events, and keep in touch with them. Understanding their preferences and priorities can help frame your proposals more effectively.

- **Maintain detailed records:** Keeping detailed records of past proposals, such as feedback received, can be very useful. It enables you to track your progress, polish your strategies, and avoid repeating past errors and mistakes.

Conclusion: Mastering the Art of Grant Proposals

With our journey coming to an end, know that it is just the beginning of your success in the dynamic realm of nonprofits. In this journey, the art of writing grant proposals will come in handy.

Mastering the art of grant proposals is a vital skill as it will help you secure funding and drive forward impactful projects. The process, though difficult and demanding, can prove to be immensely rewarding when you approach it with the right mindset and strategy.

Reflecting on this explorative journey, it becomes very clear that successful grant writing is not merely a technical skill; it is a strategic endeavor that necessitates a deeper understanding of your nonprofit's mission, the needs of the community you aim to serve, and the interests and priorities of your potential funders.

Throughout this journey, you have developed a keen sense of narrative crafting and learned how to tell compelling stories that will resonate with your grant reviewers. You need to hone your research skills to identify the ideal funding opportunities and to collect data that supports your case. The capability to present a concise, clear, and compelling argument becomes second nature, as does the meticulous attention to detail needed to meet the specific criteria and guidelines of each grant.

Additionally, the process of grant writing nurtures a culture of collaboration and continuous improvement within your organization. It encourages all team members to work together, sharing feedback and insights to refine proposals. This collaborative spirit often extends to building partnerships with other organizations, increasing the collective impact on the community.

Success in grant writing is also a testament to your commitment to the mission. Each proposal mirrors the dedication to making a positive and lasting difference and the persistence in seeking the required resources to achieve that purpose. Simply put, the journey is characterized by resilience, perseverance, and an unwavering belief in your ability to effect positive change.

Venturing on the grant-writing journey can seem daunting sometimes, but with the techniques and strategies you have learned, you are now equipped to navigate this intricate landscape. The skills you have learned are not only devices for securing funding but also keys to opening your nonprofit's full potential.

First, always remember the significance of preparation. Effective grant writing starts long before you put pen to paper. Conduct thorough research and understand your funder's priorities as well as the specific requirements of each grant.

Next, you need to embrace the power of storytelling. Every nonprofit has a unique story that echoes its values, mission, vision, and impact on the community. So, craft a compelling narrative that can capture the essence of your organization and the importance of your work. Use data and real-life examples to state the problem you are addressing and the outcomes you aim to attain. A well-told story will not only engage your reader but also create an emotional connection that can bring support.

Most importantly, do not underestimate the value of precision and clarity. Your proposal must be well-organized. Avoid overly technical language and jargon that can confuse your reader. Rather, use straightforward language to convey your ideas clearly and effectively. Ensure that your proposal is error-free and follows your funder's guidelines meticulously. Attention to detail will show your professionalism.

Collaboration is another building block of successful grant writing. Engage your team in the entire process, leveraging their expertise and perspectives. Collect input from your team, finance officers, program staff, and other stakeholders to ensure that your proposal not only stands out but is also accurate and comprehensive.

In this journey, rejection is normality. Although they are part of the grant-writing process, they must not deter you. Each application, whether it is successful or not, is your ladder toward growth and success. Seek feedback from funders when needed, and use it to adapt your approach. Continuous learning and adaptation are important components of long-term success.

Lastly, believe in your mission and the positive change you are driving. The dedication and passion you bring to your work are going to be your greatest assets. Let them shine in your proposals. Your conviction will surely resonate with funders, inspiring confidence in your organization's skill to deliver meaningful results.

As you implement the techniques and strategies learned, I encourage you to reflect on the progress and growth your organization embraces. Celebrate each milestone, both small and big, and acknowledge the collective effort that goes into each proposal. Your commitment to mastering grant writing is your testament to your commitment to bringing positive change.

In closing, I invite you to review the practices and the concepts we have covered. Consider how they can be tailored to fit your organization's unique context. Your insights are invaluable, so please consider leaving a review. Your feedback will assist many others who are eager to embark on this journey but need guidance and reassurance.

Thank you for your commitment to your mission and for striving to make a lasting difference. Together, through mastering the art of effective grant writing, we can unlock the potential to bring lasting and meaningful change in our communities.

As you continue on this journey, know that each step will bring you closer to realizing your dream and making a positive impact on your community. Embrace all the challenges, stay committed, and enjoy the process.

May your journey be filled with laughter, blessings, and ease!

References

Burnett-Thompson, A. (2020, August 8). *90% of startups fail in the first 5 years. Here's how to beat the odds.* Medium. https://drandrewbt.medium.com/90-of-startups-fail-in-the-first-5-years-heres-how-to-beat-the-odds-a8796e7089f8

Candid Foundation Directory. (n.d.). *Find grants to fund nonprofits with Foundation Directory.* https://fconline.foundationcenter.org/

Candid Learning. (n.d.). *How many nonprofit organizations are there in the U.S.?* https://learning.candid.org/resources/knowledge-base/number-of-nonprofits-in-the-u-s/

Centers for Disease Control and Prevention. (2010). *Overweight and obesity.* https://www.cdc.gov/ncbddd/disabilityandhealth/documents/obesityFactsheet2010.pdf

Charity: Water. (n.d.). *About us.* https://www.charitywater.org/uk/about

Grant, V. A. (2024, February 6). *The data on funder relationships.* Grant Professionals Association. https://grantprofessionals.org/news/662699/The-Data-on-Funder-Relationships.htm

Hoy, T. (2023, May 18). *What is a 501(c)(3) organization, and what are the different types?* BoardEffect. https://www.boardeffect.com/blog/what-are-the-different-types-of-501c3-organizations/

Hussey, D. M., Kirsop, P. L., & Meissen, R. E. (2001, September 28). Global reporting initiative guidelines: An evaluation of sustainable development metrics for industry. *Environmental Quality Management, 11*(1), 1–20. https://doi.org/10.1002/tqem.1200

Hutton, G., & Chase, C. (2017). Water supply, sanitation, and hygiene. In C. N. Mock, R. Nugent, O. Kobusingye, & K. R. Smith (Eds.), *Injury prevention and environmental health* (3rd ed.). The International Bank for Reconstruction and Development / The World Bank.

Patil, R. (2024, January 9). *Contingency funds: What are they and how much should you set aside?* Multiproject. https://multiproject.org/learningcentre/contingency-funds-what-are-they-and-how-much-should-you-set-aside/

Sheth, U. (2022, October 18). *Impact measurement challenges and its importance for nonprofits.* LinkedIn. https://www.linkedin.com/pulse/impact-measurement-challenges-its-importance-nonprofits-unmesh-sheth/

Strunk, S. L., & Bussel, J. B. (2015). The Healthy Kids, Healthy Communities National Program. *Journal of Public Health Management and Practice, 21*, S1–S3. https://doi.org/10.1097/phh.0000000000000188

Tetlow, S. (2024, April 9). *5 grant submission mistakes you can't afford to make (and how to avoid them).* Grant Engine. https://grantengine.com/5-grant-submission-mistakes-you-cant-afford-to-make-and-how-to-avoid-them/

United States Environmental Protection Agency. (2023, May 23). *Our mission and what we do.* https://www.epa.gov/aboutepa/our-mission-and-what-we-do

Universal Services Administrative Co. (n.d.). *Request for proposals (RFP) checklist.* https://www.usac.org/wp-content/uploads/rural-health-care/documents/hcf/RFP-Checklist-FINAL.pdf

www.ingramcontent.com/pod-product-compliance
Lightning Source LLC
Chambersburg PA
CBHW072052230526
45479CB00010B/682